The Red Light Runner

PRAISE QUOTES

"The word 'courage' is so often misused...certainly when talking about sports. Courage is not a bold play-call in football or a risky strategy in golf. Courage is making a choice for what's right even though you know you might suffer because of it. That perfectly describes Bobbi Lancaster. I have had the great privilege of meeting more than a few remarkable people through my four decades of reporting, and Dr. Lancaster stands prominently among that group. Her story is one of strength and true courage and this book is a must read."

Jimmy Roberts, NBC sports,
author of 'Breaking the Slump'.

"The Red Light Runner is an honest story of a life most of us can't imagine. It is a life that reinforces the importance of empathy, compassion and forgiveness for oneself and for others."

Jim Obergefell, Supreme Court plaintiff
(Obergefell vs. Hodges; marriage equality, 2015),
speaker and author of 'Love Wins'.

"Bobbi is my heroine. I pledge to demonstrate in my own life the courage that she demonstrates in hers. I am a better person because of Bobbi Lancaster and you will be too for having read this book."

Chris Dorris, speaker, success coach and
author of 'Creating Your Dream'.

"Bobbi Lancaster is a brave and courageous transgender woman. As a talented doctor, golfer and fighter for equality, this book shares her life and transition story in a funny and poignant manner. I love her unique, charming and compelling way of explaining her journey. I highly recommend this book."

Sheila Kloefkorn, CEO of KEO Marketing
Inc., former national board member of the
Human Rights Campaign.

"As a fellow competitor on the Cactus Tour, I witnessed firsthand the prejudice and obstacles Bobbi encountered in coming out and speaking out. Her decision to live a true and authentic life came at a high cost. The media scrutiny was intense and she buckled at times, but she never allowed the circumstances to break her. I don't know many people who could have handled everything with more grace and resilience. Her determination to help the transgender community is admirable and her messaging around acceptance and equality is incredibly powerful.

This book is a must read for anyone who struggles with self-acceptance, or suffers from the sting of discrimination or is simply seeking a deeper understanding of transgender issues. I am so proud to stand with Bobbi and call her my friend."

Nina Rodriguez, retired Cactus and Symetra Tour
champion professional golfer, Golf Channel Big Break
contestant, nursing student, wife and mother.

ISBN-13: 9781979034579
ISBN-10: 1979034575

The Red Light Runner

Dr. Bobbi Lancaster MD

WITH A FOREWORD BY CHRIS DORRIS

*"What did my hands do
before they held you?"*

S<small>YLVIA</small> P<small>LATH</small>

This book is dedicated to Lucy who enlisted all the king's horses and all the king's men to help put this Humpty Dumpty together again.

BY THE SAME AUTHOR

Backyard Adventures
My Friend Flutter
Fairway Secrets
The Gardener

Table of Contents

Foreword

BY CHRIS DORRIS

About twenty years ago a golf buddy referred a client to me for some mental training. At the time, that's what I did. I helped golfers train their minds in order to perform better. Dr. Bob was a physician. He was a tall, athletic, and very talented competitive golfer who had a long list of golfing success stories in his resume. He was cool. Pretty darn smart and pretty darn funny too. I had two or three sessions with this guy to help with his tournament insecurities. We did some good work and parted ways.

Fast forward fifteen years later and another competitive client of mine, a super talented senior woman golfer, referred a new client to me. She told me in advance that this person was unique and needed my help in an equally unique way. She told me that Bobbi was a transgender woman who wanted to play competitive golf and was having some real challenges both internally (emotionally) and externally (socially). So we met and got to work. Neither of us realized until our third session that we had met before. Bobbi told me she was formerly Dr. Bob, the guy I had trained all those many years ago.

We had a good laugh over that. Bobbi is about as funny as anyone I've ever met. You are about to discover that fact for yourself as you enjoy her phenomenal story telling. I'm not kidding. You're going to laugh your ass off several times in each chapter. She never takes herself too seriously. Well maybe not never.

Hers is a story that she is now able to tell with passion as she juxtaposes personal life experiences with scientific explanations. This wasn't always the case. Her story involves a tremendous amount of pain related to discrimination and rejection. This type of pain is universally experienced. Bobbi's mission is to find a solution to this suffering. She and other courageous individuals are willing to carry the torch of awareness, the torch of oneness, the torch of compassion and forgiveness to name a few. And Bobbi does this with great humility.

Transgenderism continues to be entirely misunderstood. I didn't know a darn thing about it until I met Bobbi. I was ignorant and had my own learned prejudices that I wasn't even aware of. We are all judgmental and I mean all of us. Google the word and as you type you'll see several phrases auto-populate like: "It is a mental disorder" or "transgenderism is offensive" or "it's not real." This is where we're at folks.

Just yesterday I had a client come to the office for a coaching session and he asked me what's new. I told him proudly that I've been given the honor of writing the foreword for a former client's powerful new book on her experience as a transgender woman. I saw the smirk on his face and I knew what was coming next. It was the same uninformed kind of joke I used to make before meeting Bobbi. He simply said, "Pat," and then laughed. He was referencing the androgynous character from an old Saturday Night Live skit that everyone made fun of. I'm happy to say I channeled Bobbi's spirit at that moment and responded with the same kind of graceful aplomb that she often displays. I've witnessed it first hand at my golf club when she's been confronted with a derogatory comment. I simply referenced some of the fascinating biological events that occur in the development of a fetus that explain why people are different. And he learned something; Forward progress.

Some thought-leaders today believe that we, as a species, are moving toward a quantum leap in consciousness. What that means is our next evolutionary step won't be of a physical nature but rather of a psychological one. And I hope they're right and I believe they are. People like Dr. Bobbi Lancaster are evidence of that.

These days we are becoming much more aware of the energetics of thought. Our thought emissions, so to speak, are being measured by devices like the electroencephalograph. These machines indicate the frequencies of thought and how they broadcast out and interface with the world. It can be said that at all times we are either purifying or polluting the world with our thoughts. It simply depends on the quality and the intent. Bobbi's intent is to promote a more peaceful society and to make the world a less hostile place by reminding us all that there could never be anything more divine than our truths.

As a personal transformation coach, my work involves teaching folks how to free themselves from the conditioning of their past that has caused them to settle, struggle or suffer. From the moment we are born, our conditioning begins. It serves some of us but for others, not so much. It becomes our task to identify which is which and to reprogram the beliefs that don't serve us. For example, we've all heard that prejudice is entirely learned. No child comes into this world with a mentality that they are better than someone else. We learn that. We learn to judgmentally acknowledge separateness. And that unconscious learning governs us until we become conscious of it and mindfully do the work to reprogram. Unfortunately the vast majority of us are never taught how to do that. So we go through life with these false beliefs about ourselves, many of which involve inadequacy.

Take for example the story about a little boy and his mother at a grocery store. Checking out in front of them is a very obese man. The little boy sees the unusually large man and asks his mother, in a normal speaking volume, "Mommy, why is that man so fat?" The mother is immediately horrified. She becomes flustered and turns to the man and doesn't know what to say. She faces her son and scolds him saying, "That is rude! You don't do that!" She turns back to the man and apologizes, "I am so sorry sir." Meanwhile the little boy is imprinting all of this subconsciously. He is made fully aware that he just said something terribly wrong. However he is completely unaware of exactly what he did that was so bad. He has yet to be educated about what is socially acceptable but his learning has now begun. The little guy is confused and scared. He is learning that his curiosity (his truth) is a punishable offence. He is trying to make sense of the fact that it is okay to ask why there are lots of candy and magazines at the check-out lane. And it is acceptable to ask how the conveyor belt knows when to stop all by itself. But it is not okay to ask about a persons' obesity. He then spends the rest of his self-conscious life contemplating this and many more issues as he attempts to sort out which of his truths are acceptable and which ones aren't.

None of us are exempt from this sort of conditioning. Unless attended to, it causes needless and lifelong internal conflict and stress. Now imagine in Bobbi's case complicating things further by adding into the equation the development of a gender identity center in the brain that is not in agreement with the appearance of the rest of the body. Yeah. Good luck with that. Not only does the affected individual have to deal with the usual learned self-consciousness and perceived inadequacies, they also have the added burden of being completely misunderstood. They are forced to deal with the ignorance of people like me and my previously mentioned client.

Through very painful and intensive reprogramming work, Bobbi was able to heal herself from the toxic and literally life-threatening shame she'd learned from so many sources. And now she's free to tell her story to the world, and to do so with grace and wisdom.

This book is about the trials and tribulations of a transgender woman. However it is also about the challenges that all human beings share. The issues are universal and include freeing ourselves from our past conditioning so that we can experience the beauty of life without our learned self-doubt and feelings of inadequacy and shameful self-consciousness. We all struggle to extricate ourselves from the prison of the conditioned mind. This work requires courage. It is not easy to confront conventional (uninformed) thinking and to leap into the unknown because you know it's going to hurt like hell. Abandoning the only truth, however false, a person has ever known becomes the imperative. You are about to discover that this manuscript is basically an instruction manual on how to rid yourself of needless suffering.

Bobbi is my heroine. I pledge to demonstrate in my own life the kind of courage that she demonstrates in hers. I am a better man because of Bobbi Lancaster and you too will be a better person for having read this book.

Chris Dorris is an author, speaker and success coach. He can be reached at www.christopherdorris.com.

Preface

I was busy pulling weeds in my beloved garden when I heard our new puppy, Bentley, yelping non-stop in the house. Within minutes all ten of our dogs started barking. I scraped the dirt off my shoes, wiped my hands and went to investigate the uproar. It took only a few moments to sort things out: Bentley was upset at one of the older dogs, Checkers, who'd taken his favorite toy. Now the entire pack was in turmoil because their balance had been upset.

The problem was solved by returning the stuffed animal to Bentley and distracting Checkers with a new toy. The barking stopped immediately and harmony was restored to our family of Havanese.

As I walked back to the garden, it crossed my mind there is a lot of 'barking' going on in our community at this time too. I wish it was as easy to restore balance and harmony.

In essence, this is the purpose of my book.

My mission is to change hearts and minds in an effort to promote a more peaceful society. I hope that once you have finished reading, you will want to join in my effort. Here is a very personal example to illustrate what I'm talking about.

I am one of thousands of transgender women in the United States who are being 'barked' at. It's not because we took someone's toy. It is because we are different and our mere existence upsets people. The 'fear-biting' of others takes the form of bullying, harassment, assault, marginalization and every conceivable act of discrimination. The collective damage inflicted is immeasurable and so unnecessary. We resort to hiding in an effort to avoid persecution, until we can't hide anymore.

I think everyone can identify with hiding because there is a basic human need to be loved and valued. We all want to be accepted and included and can go to considerable lengths to fit in.

I'm about to tell you all the messy details of how living in the closet almost led to my self-destruction. My survival involved family, friends, love and some degree of luck and I am fortunate to be alive.

In an effort to be helpful, I'm willingly exposing myself for all to see. My storytelling will be raw and from the heart. Hopefully the steps I finally took to live authentically will be instructive.

I am determined to address discrimination head on and reveal what it will take to stop the 'barking'. The solution needs to include honest talking, listening and education. It requires empathy and being open to change. Forgiveness and reconciliation need to play prominent roles in the healing process.

Thanks for going on this journey with me. The book is a memoir but it is so much more. I promise it will not always be serious. Along the way I'm going to provide you with information about farming and gardening, butterflies and hummingbirds, piano, professional golf, practicing medicine, the media and even flatus. While you are laughing or perhaps crying, I hope you will be spiritually moved as well.

Finally, keep this in mind. In some small way, you and I are about to make the world a less hostile place. As you turn to the first page, I'll return to my garden because the plants need water.

Enjoy.

"If there is a book that you want to read, but it hasn't been written yet, you must be the one to write it."

Toni Morrison

One

BLESS ME FATHER

As far back as I can remember I've always been in a hurry. I had the feeling I was going to die young and time was of the essence. Impatience and easy frustration were my constant companions. When I started to write this book, I had the urge to tell you right away about a life changing incident that involved an authority figure when I was fourteen.

You would have been lost. So I forced myself to slow down and take a breath because I think it's best to start where every story begins.

I was the first of four children and Rosalie and Doug Lancaster were my proud new parents. My mom had developed toxemia late in the pregnancy and she had been confined to the hospital for a week before my delivery. She was not feeling well.

My dad had been confined to a jail cell that very same week. I don't think he was feeling very well either. Finally his disgusted and disappointed parents posted bail at the last minute so he could be at my birth. It's a long story and I'll tell you about it later.

Forceps were needed to pull me out on June 23, 1950. Can you imagine what it was like back in those days? Obstetrical ultrasound had not been invented yet, so no one knew whether their baby was going to be a boy or a girl. They did not know if their child would be malformed. Even the delivery date was often a guess. There was tension in the air at every delivery, including mine.

Apparently the moment I emerged the doctor proclaimed, "It's a boy," and then quickly added, "He looks perfectly healthy." I had a red birthmark on my right cheek but that was small potatoes.

There was great relief and happiness all round. From what I've been told, my father's mom looked me up and down. She was a no-nonsense kind of person and I was her first grandchild. Finally she stated, in her matter of fact way, "He has piano fingers." Now how did she know in just a few short years, I would become a very skilled pianist?

My birth had occurred during a move to a new house. My mother and I were discharged seven days post-partum.

Arriving home from the hospital

We were greeted at the front door to unopened boxes, an empty refrigerator, a sink full of dirty dishes and disgusting, soiled laundry everywhere. If I could have talked I would have said something sarcastic like, "Thanks Dad. Thanks for organizing the new house so nicely. Are you trying to make sure I know you're an uncaring, lazy slob? If that was your goal, you have done an amazing job." My mother and father were off to a rocky start and I was along for the ride. Maybe I should have resisted the forceps and stayed in the womb a little longer.

My mom was born in 1929 at the start of the Great Depression to a French Canadian, Roman Catholic farming family. She was the third daughter to a family desperately in need of a strong son. Their disappointment was palpable. She was named Rosalie Clara Robert and Mom made it clear later in life she detested her middle name. She would say, "Cows are named Clara, not people!"

Along with her sisters, Mom worked very hard in the tobacco and sugar beet fields. On top of that, there were cucumbers and tomatoes to be picked as well. She also tended to the cows and pigs and chickens. After a family member put a bird down the front of her dress as a prank, young Rosalie developed a life-long fear of birds and anything that fluttered.

The work was back-breaking and thankless. After a full day of outdoor work she was also expected to help her mother with the indoor chores too.

Rosalie received an elementary education in a single room school in Pain Court, Ontario where she and her sister Jane taught themselves how to speak English from a book they had found. She received awards for her public speaking skills. Once she'd completed the eighth grade her parents decided there was no point in further education for her or any of their daughters.

So Rosalie, at the ripe old age of fourteen, was sent off to the nearby 'big city' of Chatham to live with relatives and work in a garment factory. She was ordered to send her earnings back to the family farm that still sported an outhouse, chamber pots, butter churns, milk separators and all the conveniences of a modern life. Horses were used instead of tractors because they were more cost effective.

Her supervisor at the factory was an officious, cold taskmaster named Millicent. They were assembling uniforms for the Second World War troops. As luck would have it, she met Doug, the seventeen year old son of her supervisor. She went to several dances with him and then he enlisted with the U.S. Army Paratroopers and went off to war.

Private Douglas Lorne Lancaster, 1944

Doug made a serious effort to stay in touch while he was away, writing almost daily love letters.

He had been born in Detroit in 1926 to a mother who was barely sixteen. The marriage had been hastily organized to avoid disgrace. After his birth the family moved across the border to Ontario, where his young parents found work in the small picturesque city of Chatham, along the Thames River.

Because he had been the reason for the hurried nuptials, there is not much evidence that Doug was ever truly welcomed or loved by his parents. He contracted polio when he was in his early teens and it weakened his legs. Apparently he developed a very powerful upper body to compensate. Eventually he recovered the full use of his lower extremities.

Doug attended high school where he was described as a very bright student. He enjoyed building motorized model airplanes using balsam wood and was always in the company of his dog, Mickey. Then he met the pretty young farm girl called Rosalie and before you knew it, he went off to war. Remember, he was seventeen and his 'girlfriend' was just fourteen.

I always wondered why he enlisted to be a para-trooper. I found documentation that said he was a sharp-shooter and that he had served as a drill sergeant too. At the conclusion of the war, he returned to Chatham where he continued to date the farm girl.

Rosalie, 1944

Rosalie and Doug were married in 1948. Her father was absolutely opposed to the marriage because his daughter was marrying an Englishman and, even worse, a Protestant. Since the formation of the country over 150 years ago, there has been a tension between English and French Canadians. The cause is deeply rooted in religious differences and obvious language and cultural barriers. Rosalie's dad was caught up in this acrimony. Legend has it he arrived at the wedding completely drunk and made a farce of the ceremony.

The newlyweds moved to a rental apartment in the Anglo community of Chatham, about twenty miles from my mother's childhood farm. For her, it might as well have been on a different continent. As an outsider she experienced predictable difficulties fitting in. Not only was she French but Rosalie was also considered unsophisticated because she was from the country.

It would appear that Mom did everything she could to blend in and keep a low profile. She never spoke French unless she was visiting the farm and talking to her parents and siblings.

I loved to hear her speak in her native tongue because she appeared to come alive. Even though I could not understand a word she was saying at the farm, Mom was always smiling and animated.

Me at five months of age

In 1952, two years after I came along, my brother Ron was born. This perfect little baby boy would grow up to be an acclaimed mathematician and teacher. However Ron and my mom would soon become punching bags for my frustrated father.

My dad was a very bright fellow and enjoyed building things, just like his father. Doug gradually assembled an impressive collection of tools and had many hobbies such as stamp collecting and playing golf. He was well liked and had many friends.

However there was a troubling side to his personality. Doug was easily frustrated and quick to anger. Like his father and many of the men on the Lancaster side of the family, he drank excessively.

On looking back, I have come to the conclusion that he never knew unconditional love when he was a youngster and I believe he tried to self-soothe with alcohol as he grew older. I also think he found himself trapped by the obligations of providing for a young family. On top of that Doug was working at jobs that were too mundane given his intelligence. However they were all he could find given the lack of advanced training and his arrest record.

I told you he was in jail the week before my delivery. He had been charged with assault and he eventually pled guilty to a lesser offence and received probation. Of course he had to report this event on every job application he completed. It became his personal 'ball and chain' and likely contributed to depression and the nervous breakdowns he struggled with from time to time throughout his entire life.

To his credit, my dad did not run away from the responsibilities of Rosalie, Ron and me. He soldiered on dutifully, though at times his internal conflicts reached the boiling point and he would erupt like a volcano.

Doug would pick fights with friends and strangers alike. He would injure loved ones and say things that were extremely hurtful. These episodes were loud and violent and fueled by self-hate. Eventually these eruptions would subside and then apologies and promises would be made. This cycle would repeat over and over. Even during the calm spells, there was fear and tension that permeated our 'happy' little home in Chatham.

Looking back I could fill my entire book with memories of this small idyllic town. I remember horse-drawn carriages delivering ice, milk and bread to our door. I recall a man with a shovel following the horses to scoop up the poop littering the street. I remember the town knife sharpener ringing his bell as he pushed his cart along the sidewalk.

However the memory I most clearly recall was seeing my dad explode during one of his rages. He chased my mom around the kitchen table and hit her. I was so small but I jumped up to help her and said, "No Dad. Please stop!" He yelled at me to sit down and then he hit me in the head so hard that my mind went blank.

I was stunned but once recovered, I remember promising myself I would hurt him back someday for this.

Learning to walk as a one year old

Uneasy Rider

Me and my dad

We moved to Ridgetown, Ontario in 1955 because my father found a better job at a small metal stamping company. This community, with a population of two thousand people, was about an hour drive from Chatham. It was right in the middle of farm country. There was an agricultural college at the edge of town, a golf course nearby and Rondeau Park on the Lake Erie shore where I first learned to swim.

My sister Sandy joined the family in 1956. My dad called her Princess and said she was the twinkle in his eye. I remember wishing I had a nice nickname like that. Sometimes he called me Butch but I really did not like that name. Sandy was so pretty and delicate that I felt protective of her.

My parents enrolled me in grade one of the Catholic school and I walked the mile and a half to the two room school every day. I also served mass as an altar boy at St. Michael's Church. At the time my dad was attending mass too and he completed a training program and converted to Catholicism. I vaguely remember his baptism and it struck me as being odd because, up to that point, I had only seen babies get baptized.

By now, I was eight years old and doing all the usual things a little boy does. I had a paper route and played every sport including soccer, baseball and hockey. I was a little track and field star and won all the ribbons.

During my free time I also searched for empty pop bottles on the side of the road. People would buy a Coke for 5 cents and drink it in their car. They would finish it in a couple of minutes and throw the empty out the window as they sped from town. I would find the bottles in the ditch and redeem them for 2 cents each at the local store. This cash supplemented my paper route money.

From time to time my dad would ask me for a 'loan' to help pay for family bills. I was so proud to be able to hand my father some money. These loans were never repaid, though they were forgiven a very long time ago.

Eight years of age

I fell in love for the first time with Mary Flood. We were in second grade and she had the prettiest smile and the most gorgeous pigtails. We would talk about things at recess and even exchanged Valentine Day cards. One day I summoned my courage and gave her a little kiss on the cheek. Sister Mary Louise was one of the teachers at the school and she witnessed the kiss. She scolded me.

Later that same week, we had a school assembly. We sang God Save the Queen and learned about Elmer the Safety Elephant. Then, to my surprise, Sister Mary Louise called me up on stage. She told the entire school that she had caught me kissing a girl and this sort of behavior was not acceptable.

Next Sister Edna, the school principal, appeared and addressed the students and announced I had to be punished. Now I was really getting scared and remember trembling. I thought I was going to get 'the strap' and was worried they were going to call my parents. I would really be in serious trouble then.

At that point the principal did something strange. She reached into a bag and handed me a doll and told me for the next week, I had to carry the doll with me at all times during the school day. If I felt the urge to kiss anyone, I was instructed to kiss the doll instead. I was ordered to pick the doll up at her office every morning and drop it off at the end of classes. Naturally everyone laughed at me and I was humiliated. On looking back, the punishment was more than a little sadistic but thankfully I did not get the strap.

Mercifully that awful week came to an end. I had weathered the teasing and the jeers even though it had been beyond embarrassing. Nonetheless I found out just how tough I could be.

I never did talk to Mary Flood again, but I still have the school photo she gave me on the back of which she wrote, "I love you."

This was the first of several public humiliations that took place during my formative years. They contributed to intense anxiety and fear later in life when I had to perform in front of others.

Thankfully my parents never found out about this episode. I finally told my mom this story a couple of years ago while we were sharing our life secrets. I never kissed a girl again until I met my wife-to-be when I was twenty years old.

❖ ❖ ❖

During this time my father was always busy with work, his friends and hobbies. There was a lot of pool, poker and golf consuming his free time and all of it involved drinking. He was altogether not present, especially emotionally. His parenting style was a continuation of his drill sergeant training. Ron and I would literally have to march in to the room and stand at attention when he called us. We would have to say, "Yes sir," and "No sir," in response to his orders.

On the other hand, my mother was always there. She did her best to keep us happy and healthy and she was the epitome of sacrifice and unconditional love for her children.

Mom would patch the holes in our clothes and mend our socks. When the upper part of my old shoe separated from the sole, she gave me a red rubber ring from the lid of her canning jar to place over the toe of the shoe. It held the two parts together and thankfully stopped the embarrassing flapping for a few more miles. She showed me how to place newspaper inside my shoe to 'patch' a hole in the sole. This prevented my sock from sticking through the hole and wearing out too.

My mom would make us 'exotic' sugar or mustard sandwiches. She would take a slice of white bread with no butter and sprinkle a little sugar on one side of it. Or she would just spread a small amount of mustard on a dry piece of bread. Then she would cut the bread into five pieces that she called 'fingers'. It would make the meal look larger than it really was. We actually begged for these sandwiches. She also served us bologna in so many creative ways and made it feel like a special treat.

The truth of the matter was we were almost out of food and she was making ends meet.

I did not know we were poor and just scraping by because I had nothing to compare it with. However one thing became certain: I wanted to help with the food shortage because I was hungry.

I took it upon myself to wander the fields near our home and collect wild fruits and vegetables from abandoned old farms. My mother used everything I brought home. I also asked her to teach me how to plant a garden. She would use the vegetables from my small plot to feed the family too.

In spite of this, I still went to bed hungry some nights. My stomach would be really noisy but I was not brave enough to get up and go to the kitchen to ask for food. That would involve facing my father who was finally home after an evening of drinking. So my mother and I worked out a system. I would clear my throat loudly twice and she would hear me from her room. This signaled I was hungry. Then she would bring me a cracker or a cookie to make the hunger go away. Or she would just rub my back until I went to sleep.

She took care of our medical needs too. She gave us weekly castor oil and vitamin drops. Mom applied mercurochrome to our cuts and scrapes and mustard or onion poultices to our chests to treat respiratory infections.

In spite of her care, I still got all the childhood illnesses prevalent at the time. I was also skinny and knobby-kneed and there was concern about rickets. Unfortunately I had asthma too and sometimes I could barely breathe. That was scary.

Of course I was not allowed to have an indoor dog or a cat because it would make my asthma worse. I did have an outdoor cat named Mittens but he died after being hit by a car.

I had lots of dental cavities because there was no fluoride in the town water. Also, six permanent teeth never appeared after my primary teeth fell out. As a result I had a lot of spaces between my existing teeth. Too much time was spent at the dentist's office where Dr. Taylor painfully drilled my cavities out using a foot pedal to power his drill.

One day when I was about seven and Ron was five, it was time to get our tonsils out. Dr. Murphy served as the town family doctor and I recall hearing that, during the Second World War, he had been a decorated army surgeon. However he had been injured and a metal plate had been placed in his head. As a result, he experienced some motor difficulties that forced him to give up his surgical career. But those setbacks did not stop him from becoming our revered, small town doctor.

He arrived at our house with a big black bag and organized all of his instruments in preparation for the procedure. He instructed my brother to lie down on the kitchen table while the whole family watched. He then placed an ether soaked rag on his face and put him to sleep. At that point he removed his tonsils and Ron woke up with no recollection of the surgery. Ron did well.

When it was my turn, I climbed up on the table. The ether smelled very peculiar. I woke up after the procedure with a terrible sore throat and then I started gagging and coughing and spluttering. I vomited a frightening amount of blood all over the room. The operation had resulted in uncontrollable bleeding in my throat.

I remember police sirens, a speeding car and being held by my mother in the back seat of our family car. I drifted in and out of consciousness during the hour long drive to the hospital in Chatham where I had been born. From all reports, I was close to death.

"Wake up, young Robbie. Wake up. Open your eyes!" Finally it registered that someone was calling out to me. I opened my eyes and squinted because it was so bright. There was a room full of nuns in white habits and a tube in my arm with red stuff running into my body. Later I was told they were nurses, not nuns.

The bleeding had been stopped. I was weak but I was definitely back in business.

❖ ❖ ❖

A side from almost dying and kissing girls and delivering newspapers, I also devoted a great deal of time collecting and studying insects. I was absolutely enthralled with butterflies. Their quiet beauty and amazing metamorphosis intrigued me. By the time I was eight, I had a microscope, a net and several books. For the next several years I was a very busy junior entomologist, visiting neighborhood homes with the best flower gardens to look for butterflies.

My first reference book

I talked to the bees in those gardens and talked to the plants as well. I sensed they were all listening and could understand me.

One day there was a hummingbird that was also visiting the flowers and I reflexively stuck out my finger. To my utter amazement the hummingbird landed on my finger. We looked at each other for at least a minute. As far as I knew this did not happen to ordinary people. I felt very special and I thought there might be something magical about me.

On another occasion I caught a moth I could not identify. It appeared to be from the Under Wing family. There was no picture of it anywhere in my rather simple books and that's when my father did a very kind thing. He found out there was an entomologist at the college in town and arranged a meeting.

We went together and I presented the moth to the professor. He consulted the biggest books I had ever seen in my whole life and finally turned to me and said, "Robbie...I think you have found a specimen that has never been discovered before. It is very rare and I think we should name it after you."

I was beyond excited and felt so special. He then asked me how I killed my specimens before examining them. I told him I stuck a pin in their thorax. He did not approve and asked my father if I could be supplied with a real professional killing jar. When my dad agreed the professor handed me a large glass jar with a lid so big I needed two hands to unscrew it. There was a thick white paste at the bottom and it was covered with a layer of cotton batting. I was told to hold my breath when I opened the jar to place a specimen inside and to close the lid quickly. It was imperative no one else ever touch my jar. I listened carefully because I was very responsible for my age. As we left the office my father asked what was in the white paste and the professor paused, took off his glasses, looked at my father and said, "Cyanide."

Now how many eight year old kids in this day and age would be trusted with cyanide at home? Not unexpectedly the bottle would lose its effectiveness over time. So I would place it in the newspaper carrier mounted on my bike and peddle several miles to the agricultural college. The professor would add some fresh cyanide paste and I would peddle back home. Goodness knows what would have happened if I'd fallen off my bike and smashed the glass bottle. I would love to meet this educator again and ask him what he saw in me that convinced him I would be safe with cyanide. He must have been breaking some rules and I'm glad he did.

Before leaving my butterflies, I have to tell you about my net. We could not afford to buy a new one so my father decided to make it himself. The handle was from an old broom. The large round 'mouth' was made from a thick gauge, twisted wire that he firmly attached to the handle. The netting itself was made from white drapery material and it was long and strong. The goal was to catch butterflies but I could have caught dogs.

One day I left the house to go look for specimens. As I was walking down the sidewalk, I heard our screen door slam. I turned to see my little sister running toward me. Sandy was not even two years old and she wanted to come with me. Sandy was my little buddy.

To my horror, she did not have a stitch of clothes on. I was mortified and had to hide her from public view. So, I scooped her up with the net and carried her back to the house. Maybe Dad had anticipated a moment just like that when he constructed my military grade butterfly net.

Come to think of it, he built many things, including a boat, in his own very rigid and indestructible style. Upon completion of every project, he would always step back and look at the finished item and declare, "Well, that's not going anywhere."

I don't know whatever became of my net, but wherever it is now, I guarantee it is not broken.

My young life continued to unfold. I started piano lessons when I was nine and quickly became very accomplished. I was placed in the Royal Conservatory of Music program and roared through the different grades. I could express my feelings through this instrument and when I played, the tension in our home would disappear. Christmas songs would make everyone happy so I would play them often, even in July.

My piano teacher entered me in competitions and recitals. I don't recall ever winning but finished second a few times. I remember a competition in London, Ontario where I was playing a selection by Chopin. There was a very slow and quiet section and the audience was hushed as I leaned way over to my right to strike a solitary note. It was almost out of reach and as I stretched my small 9 year old frame, I farted! Yes, I passed some very nervous gas. This unwanted note reverberated off the wooden bench and echoed throughout the hall for all to hear. Everyone started laughing, including the judges. I turned beet red and lost my composure. I finished my selection, slinked off the stage and received low marks for my performance.

However, the judges did mention they enjoyed the woodwind accent I had added to the score!

Something else really special happened during those Ridgetown years. My father asked me to go to the golf course with him and caddy. I will never know what possessed him because I had never been to the course before and knew nothing about golf. However it was a chance to be with my dad.

The place was so green and quiet. The smell of the freshly cut grass was one of the most pleasant things I had ever experienced. There were birds, squirrels, butterflies and ground hogs everywhere and even a fox ran across the fairway!

Most of all, there was my dad. And he was smiling. I watched him and his buddies swing on the first hole. I could not follow the ball in flight because it went too fast. On the second hole, my father hit and everyone started jumping and hollering. He had just made his very first hole-in-one and I was there to witness it. I was considered a good luck charm from that day forward.

On that special day my dad just kept smiling and smiling like never before. Everyone was so happy and he could not wait to get home and tell Mom about his great shot.

That was the start of my love affair with the game of golf. It became the only place where I could connect with my father.

He gave me a few cut-down clubs and I taught myself by watching other people play at the public golf course. I imitated the best players. My father bragged about me and how straight I could hit the ball. I became very accomplished and played better than all the other young golfers.

By now I was 10 years old and beginning to feel I was someone special. I was brimming with confidence. I could master anything I focused on and had lots of plans. I dreamed of being a biologist or maybe a champion golfer....the best in the world. On the other hand, maybe I could be a concert pianist or perhaps a priest or a doctor and help people. I remember how powerfully I believed in myself and knew I would do something amazing in the future. There was no doubt about it. The sky was the limit.

Up to that point, I had done all the usual things a little boy does, except for one thing.

I liked to dress in girl's clothes.

I knew all along I was really a girl on the inside and my name was Bobbi. I prayed every day that God would change me into a girl just like He could turn a caterpillar into a beautiful butterfly.

When I was three or four years old I used to watch my mom get dressed to go out with my dad. I wanted to look just like her. I would wear her earrings or her necklace and feel pretty with them on.

When we moved to Ridgetown, there was a neighbor my age called Crystal. She became my very best friend even though she liked to eat worms on the sidewalk after it rained. She even ate the leg off my pet turtle and it died. I forgave her because that's what friends do. I think she must have been having some emotional problems.

It all started so innocently. Whenever I went to Crystal's house, I would ask to wear her skirt or blouse or even her shoes. It was so much fun and it felt comfortable. She had a hat I liked to put on too. I felt like her girlfriend when I was with her and I was happy and pretty and natural. That's all I remember feeling at the time. I also wanted to jump rope with her and her friends, especially Double Dutch and I wanted to play hop scotch with them too. I was never bold enough to join in.

I used to look at the majorettes in the local Santa Claus Parade and really wanted to march with them and twirl the baton. I especially wanted their white boots with tassels.

As I got a little older, I learned some grown men liked to dress as women and entertain people by singing and dancing in shows. It was called cross-dressing and they were drag queens. I also heard about a soldier who changed from a man to a woman but I wasn't sure how it had happened.

From time to time some of the grownups at the golf course and even some of my coaches would talk about queers, drag queens, fags, homos and perverts and it sounded like they hated these people. They enunciated the words with contempt. They practically spit them out. It scared me because I thought I was going to end up being one of those people they seemed to hate. I decided to keep this cross-dressing thing to myself. I especially did not want my father to find out because I suspected he shared the same aversion to fags that everyone else appeared to have. I feared he would be mad at me.

So I never talked about it and hoped Crystal would not tell her parents either. But whenever the opportunity arose, I would wear something feminine in private. It might be a dress, a skirt or a blouse when I was staying over at one of my many cousins' homes. I was always looking for an opportunity to look a little like the girl I knew I was and I continued to pray to God for a miracle.

"What do you mean we are moving? You can't be serious. I am begging you. Please do not do this. Mom, please say something to Dad and talk him out of it. I can't leave Crystal and my other friends. I can't leave the butterflies and my hummingbird friend. My cat and my turtle and my pet rabbit are all buried here. My garden is here. Please don't do this to me!"

It did not matter how much I protested. My parents had decided to move far away to a big city called Hamilton. Dad said he would make a lot more money and there would be more opportunity for all of us. The day, in 1960, that we left our two-story house on Erie street was the saddest day of my young life.

We moved to Ancaster, Ontario for a brief time and then to our new house in Hamilton. We were now three hours from my mother's farm near Chatham but it felt like we were a million miles away. There was nothing I could do except move forward and try my best.

During this disruption my mom brought a beautiful baby brother home. His name was Ken and it was love at first sight. I helped my mom with his feeding and diaper changes and dusted and cleaned the house too. I mowed the lawn and trimmed the bushes. In fact, I did most of the outdoor things my father should have been doing because he had found new drinking buddies and card games. I was known as 'Little Dad' around the house.

Aside from this I was having trouble at school. It was so much larger and there were a number of boys a lot bigger than me. They could run faster and jump higher. When it came to sports, I was no longer the big fish in a tiny pond, if you know what I mean. I found a job as a caddy at a local private golf course and continued my piano studies with a new teacher. She was the hairiest woman I had ever seen but it didn't matter because she was nice and allowed me to play contemporary music along with the classics. I also became an altar server at our new church and ultimately became the lead altar boy.

Bob, Ron and little Kenny, 1963

Yes, I was still cross-dressing secretly whenever I could and I was still praying that He would somehow turn me in to a girl. However I was losing hope because puberty was starting and I was getting taller and facial hair was appearing. My voice was cracking too. Other boys my age were excited about these changes but I found them discouraging.

During this time, my best buddy was Virgilio. He was much bigger and stronger than me and he acted as my protector because I was being teased at school. He did not have any tolerance for bullying and I was being called a teacher's pet and a brown-noser. I had the highest grades in my class and when-ever there was a recital or choir practice, I was always asked to play the piano. One year the drama teacher awarded me the lead in the school play. I participated in organized hockey and football and became a great field goal kicker and punter because Virgilio taught me these skills. You see, he was a terrific soccer player and he knew how to kick a ball.

I was not popular and I never really understood why. I had good marks, I could play the piano, I was good at sports and I wasn't ugly. However other than Virgilio, I had no other close friends. Several girls in grade 8 liked me but they were not the ones I had crushes on and I was just too awkward and self-conscious to approach them.

One cold winter day I was walking home from school when a group of boys ran up from behind me. They pushed me down and held me while they rubbed snow in my face and shoved it under my shirt. They called me a fag. I never knew why because there was no way they could have known I cross-dressed. I felt so powerless and Virgilio was nowhere to be seen. They laughed and ran off and I got up and dusted the snow from my clothes. I felt so weak and violated.

I went home and cried and listened to my favorite song over and over. It was called 'Mr. Lonely' by Bobby Vinton. I did tell Virgilio about the incident and he wanted to go and kick their asses. I told him not to do that because I sensed it would have made things worse.

Virgilio was an excellent student, a very good chess player and he wanted to be a priest. He was the oldest child and just like me, he had two brothers and a sister. I loved to go to his home because it was always so noisy and happy. His mother appeared to be constantly cooking pasta, sauces and pizzas and the aroma in their home was out of this world. His father built houses for a living and made red wine when he wasn't working. They spoke Italian and it had such a melodious sound. I often wished my home was as happy as my friend's and that my mother spoke French to me at least some of the time. In my opinion, French sounded just as beautiful as Italian.

❖ ❖ ❖

When I was fourteen years old I won the prestigious Caddy Championship at the storied Hamilton Golf and Country Club.

I was so happy and proud of my achievement. I won against much older and bigger fellows, but my celebration was tempered because I had recently proven myself to be a coward. Let me explain.

In Canada, on the third weekend of May, everyone celebrates Victoria Day in honor of the Queen of England who was in power at the time of Canadian Confederation in 1867. Traditionally most people go to a fireworks display. We waited all day for my dad to return home from golfing so he could drive the family to the park for the festivities. He came home late and

very drunk. We piled into the car even though we knew the show would be half over. I was sitting in the back seat behind my father when he became angry that all the parking spots were taken.

My mom said something to him like, "Well, if you had come home earlier, we would have easily found a spot." Suddenly and without a word, he hit her in the head. He hit her so hard her head bounced off the passenger window. He hit her again. And I did nothing. Oh, I clenched my fists and I fixed my jaw and I readied myself to hit him in the back of his head. But I held back.

I did nothing to defend my mom even though I was a young teenager and pretty strong for my age. I have never felt more ashamed and disappointed in myself and I still think about my lack of courage to this day. My mother's face swelled like a balloon. She was terribly bruised and did not leave the house for days. I could barely look at her. I never liked fireworks again.

❖ ❖ ❖

At about that same time, I was becoming more and more desperate to talk to someone about my secretive cross- dressing. The only person I felt comfortable approaching was Father Keegan, the parish priest. It would have to be somewhere safe and private, like the darkness of a confessional. The booth was familiar to me because I served as the lead altar boy at the church. It had a welcoming smell of incense. I really did not have any sins to confess so I made some up. Come to think of it, maybe concocting sins was a sin unto itself?

So there I was on that fateful day, preparing to talk with him about being Bobbi. I arrived early for confession. I was third in line. I rehearsed what I would say. My hands were sweating and ice cold.

Now I was second in line. My heart was starting to thump. There was still time for me to bolt out the door but I had to talk to the priest. I thought about disguising my voice.

I was silently freaking out as I went over and over what I would say. The parishioner in front of me was taking a long time and this prolonged the agony.

At last it was my turn. I entered the booth, closed the door behind me and waited for the priest to slide open the little partition. I felt like I was running out of air. I could hear the muffled conversation of another sinner in the opposite booth. Then there was silence and suddenly the partition opened between me and Father Keegan. I could barely see his silhouette in the darkness but I could sense his presence.

I swallowed hard and said, "Bless me Father for I have sinned. It has been one month since my last confession and these are my sins. I swore twice, disobeyed my parents once and forgot to return a library book on time." After a brief pause, he was starting to reply when I interrupted him and said, "Father, there is something that is really troubling me and I need your help.

"I have always felt like I was a girl. I secretly dress in girls clothes whenever I can. I have asked God to turn me into a girl. Do you know anything about this? Can you help me because I am desperate and confused? I need answers."

Father remained quiet. I could hear him breathing and adjusting his seating position. "My son" he said, "Your thoughts about being a girl are wrong. In fact you are committing a very big sin when you pray for these things and dress like a girl." Then he quoted something from Genesis, Leviticus and Corinthians. I did not know what he was talking about.

I was speechless as I tried to digest what he had said. Then his message finally registered. He was calling me sinful and telling me I was a bad person. Father gave me a big penance and closed the partition door with a thump. And that was that.

I was stunned. I was numb.

I wobbled out of the confessional and looked around. There was a long line of people waiting. Could anyone else have heard our conversation? I did not kneel down and say my big penance because I knew if I knelt too long, others would guess I had done something really wrong. I left the church and pedaled my bike home.

Halfway there, I got mad. How could I be a bad person? I was trying to be perfect for my parents and teachers and had the best marks in my class. I was helping my mother and caring for my little brother while at the same time being kind to the bees, the butterflies and the hummingbird. I was always assisting old people in the neighborhood who could not clear their snow or rake their leaves. I was teaching Sunday school catechism to the young children in the parish and regularly serving Mass, always on time. I was doing the chores around our house inside and out and even planted a garden to help feed our family. And I 'loaned' my father money.

How could I be a bad person?

I was crushed and never did do that penance. There was no point because I couldn't stop thinking about being Bobbi. I was sinning over and over and over with my continued, ever more secretive cross-dressing. I was going to hell and there was no doubt about it.

My life changed that day. Now the sky was no longer the limit. Being told there was something wrong with me was so hurtful and I felt hopeless.

I was doomed.

*"I write to understand as much
as to be understood."*

ELIE WIESEL

Two

THE RED LIGHT INCIDENT

I was fourteen years old and had been told I was a sinful person. I did not want anyone else to find out there was something really wrong with me, so I decided to hide. It's called being in the closet. Over the course of this chapter I want you to experience what this entailed.

When you boil it all down, I hid because I did not want to disgrace my family and embarrass myself. We would all have been the focus of gossip, name-calling and worse. I would have been bullied and teased and maybe beat up. Even at that young age, I had already observed the cruel treatment directed at people who were different.

Equally important, I did not want to disappoint my father and make him angry. I had witnessed his temper and I was scared of him. I felt like I had spent my entire life trying to win his approval and I was not about to blow it by announcing I was a girl.

I know my mom would have listened in a very loving and supportive way and she would have had a confrontation with Dad over me. There would have been arguing and someone would have been hurt. It would have been her.

Maybe others in my situation would have been more courageous and told their parents. I was not that brave.

I did try to learn more about why I felt like a girl but I could not find any books in the public library that addressed my firmly held belief.

Sometimes I closed my eyes and played make believe. I pictured walking hand in hand with my parents to a therapy session where we would learn so much about me and receive great advice. Mom and Dad would be very supportive and I would be their incredible first daughter. Dad would give me an affectionate nickname and he would say I was the 'twinkle in his eye' too.

However this was just a fantasy. There were no therapists like this in the 1950's and 1960's. There was not even a word to describe young people like me back then.

At about this time, I started secondary school and enrolled at Cathedral Boys' High School where I was taught by Jesuit priests. They were highly educated and terrific teachers and they were also strict disciplinarians. I excelled academically but I disliked being around boys all the time. I found the locker room to be full of disgusting male odors and even more disgusting talk about girls.

My buddy Virgilio did not enroll at Cathedral with me because he had other plans. He left for Chicago to attend a Jesuit seminary and begin the long preparation needed to become a priest. We exchanged letters over the years but, ever so gradually, we fell out of touch. I am getting ahead of myself as usual but I want you to know he never did finish seminary school. Years later I learned he had married and died suddenly of a heart attack when he was just 39 years old!

Cathedral Girls High School was just down the street from the Boys school and enrollment there was on my wish list. It was one more bus stop along the route and yet it might as well have been in another province. It was out of my reach.

I made new friends and they were both Italians too, like Virgilio. Their names were Rocco and Joe. They were also top students and very good athletes. They were very caring individuals and easy to talk to. Of course neither of them had any idea I was thinking about being a girl all the time. On several occasions I came close to telling them, but I was always worried about the fallout.

I gradually accumulated some female clothing and used my caddy earnings and babysitting money to purchase a skirt and a blouse. I was too embarrassed to purchase intimate clothing for myself but where there is a will, there is a way.

I wrote a note and made it look like it was from my mother. It instructed the clerk at a local department store to find a bra and panty set for my mom that was being advertised in the newspaper. The note introduced me as her son and went on to say I would pay for the articles and bring them home to her. The clerk put the piece of paper down and looked at me skeptically over the top of her glasses. My heart was beating so fast I thought she might be able to hear it.

Then she walked away and reappeared several minutes later after she'd collected the items in their correct sizes. I was shaking and fumbled with my wallet to pay her in cash. I walked briskly out of the store sensing the clerk was watching in a very knowing way until I was out of sight. She would never see me in that store again.

Once home I hid my purchase and waited for a time when I was alone. The day finally arrived and I put on my complete female outfit and combed my hair like a girl. I felt so pretty and natural and especially calm. It was such a relief to finally just be Bobbi. While wearing this attire I did my homework and practiced the piano. This routine was repeated many times during my high school years.

I was constantly on the lookout for my parents or siblings to come home unexpectedly. Sometimes I would hear a car door slam and, in a panic, race to the bathroom and lock the door. I would change quickly to my Bob clothes and hide my outfit.

The feeling I was sneaking around and doing something wrong was constant. I was meticulously careful to avoid detection but sometimes the urge to go outside as Bobbi and be validated and accepted was very strong. However the risk was too great.

I gradually became bolder and would bring my bra and panties in my brief case to school, but only if there was no gym class scheduled that day. I would put them on in a public restroom stall at the Hamilton Bus Terminal near my school, having made certain I wore a bulky sweater on those days. The entire exercise was very secretive but it made me happy because, in a small way, I was dressing like a girl.

Anxiety was my middle name because I feared a classmate might touch my back and feel a bra strap. Or there might be an unexpected physical-education class necessitating changing into my gym clothes.

One day I spied a strange looking man with a moustache and slicked-back hair looking over the bathroom stall at the bus terminal as I was putting on my lingerie. I was so scared. He was trying to get into my cubicle, so I ran out and pushed him aside forcefully. I did not stop running for a long time. I never used the restroom at the terminal again but I used to see him hanging around there.

Through it all, I studied hard and maintained my standing as one of the top students. I captained the high school golf team to the city championship. In fact I was also winning more than a few junior tournaments. and this was a huge source of pride for me.

I was on the track and field team as well and eventually could high jump six feet using a Western Roll technique. The landing area was a pit filled with sawdust. I could run like the wind and I could run forever. I still played hockey, football and soccer but they were becoming a little too rough for me. I was on the chess team and I was still in love with my beloved piano.

Just reading the above list makes me exhausted. I forgot to mention I was still working as a caddy and I had a regular babysitting job for neighbors across the street. Back then I had so much energy.

I must tell you about the babysitting because it is evidence of how much I was trusted and respected in my community. To begin with, it was very unusual for a young boy to babysit. In spite of this, the Smiths asked me to care for their two young daughters every couple of weeks while they attended concerts and the theater. I felt honored. The girls were 5 and 7 years of age and they were adorable. Their names were Penny and Samantha respectively.

I would play doll house with them and read story books like Winnie the Pooh and Green Eggs and Ham. I would ad lib during the readings and they would laugh so hard. It encouraged me to behave in an even more silly way. Then I would get them ready for bed, tuck them in and sing their favorite lullabies. I loved watching them sleep and dreamed of having my own children someday.

Besides this, I volunteered in every way possible and did whatever I could to help the community. It made me feel good. Also, even though I was sinning all the time by surreptitiously being Bobbi, I thought God would notice my good deeds and spare me from going to hell.

Now I want to tell you about an absolutely terrible incident that happened to me during my first year of high school. Frankly I think being banished to hell would have been easier.

It had been a long day of classes and after extra-curricular activities I had missed the bus. I walked home in the dark and arrived as the dinner dishes were being cleaned. After completing my homework, I was exhausted and went to bed.

At around eleven o'clock, I was suddenly awakened. Someone was shaking me and when I turned over in bed, I could see the silhouette of my father standing over me in the darkness. He ordered me to come to the kitchen immediately. I followed him and remember squinting as I adjusted to the bright overhead light. My mom was already seated anxiously at the table. I sat down between the two of them.

My dad appeared upset as he looked me directly in the eye and said, "Bob, we know what's been going on but we want you to tell us all about it in your own words. And don't beat around the bush. I am not in the mood for any lies."

I was stunned and started to shake. Had my parents somehow found out about my cross-dressing? Had they discovered my hidden stash of girls' clothes? Oh my God! I was really in big trouble now. I had been so incredibly careful to hide and never once slipped up. I could not believe they had discovered my deeply held secret?

Was this the moment I had to tell them about feeling like a girl? Or should I just keep my mouth shut and play dumb? What should I do? My mind was racing and I was having trouble thinking straight. I was in full panic mode.

Finally I took a chance and lied. "I don't know what to say to you, Dad, because I don't know what you're talking about."

He looked angry, leaned toward me and said in a threatening voice, "Bob, this is your last chance. Tell me what you have been up to and tell me right now or else you're going to be in even bigger trouble."

Now I was really scared and felt a tear running down my face. In spite of his intimidation I still chose to hide.

"Dad, please don't hurt me. I really don't know what you're talking about."

I braced myself for the inevitable blow and began to cower when my mom exclaimed, "Doug, he's telling the truth! Can't you see he is telling the truth? He doesn't know! He doesn't know!"

My father calmed down but I was a trembling mess. He cleared his throat and said, "Okay Bob. Pay attention while I spell things out for you. An hour ago we got a call from a neighbor two blocks away and they were really upset. Apparently they saw you standing in front of their house exposing yourself. They said you were masturbating and even though it was dark outside, they were sure it was you. They wanted us to know they had called the police." Dad looked directly at me to assess my reaction.

I was stunned. No, maybe dumbfounded was a better description. I was speechless. On the one hand I was glad I had not told them about being Bobbi. But on the other hand, I was really upset someone had accused me of doing something so gross.

I finally found my voice and said emphatically to Mom and Dad, "I don't know those neighbors very well but they have definitely mistaken me for someone else because never in a million years would I do something like that." I repeated this statement again even more stridently.

Dad studied me from head to toe. Then he closed his eyes for about a minute and deliberated his next move. Finally he spoke very slowly and quietly.

"I believe you, Bob. We are going to get to the bottom of this mess in the morning. Now go to bed."

I was so relieved, gave them a big hug and went back to my bedroom. I could not sleep at all.

The next day, while preparing to leave for school, the phone rang and my mother answered. It was the police and they wanted to arrange a time to speak with my parents.

Then the phone rang again and it was the Smiths, my babysitting clients. They told my parents that a neighbor had informed them of my behavior and they were very disappointed in me. The Smiths made it clear I was no longer going to be their babysitter. I was crushed.

It was now highly likely that the entire neighborhood knew about me, the local pervert. Nothing travels faster than the speed of light, except gossip.

I left for school with my brown briefcase in hand and walked down the street to the bus stop two blocks away. I felt like everyone was looking out their front windows and talking about me. I just wanted to evaporate but I held my head up high and looked straight ahead. The rest of the day was a blur.

I arrived back home to learn the police had indeed talked to my parents and informed them they had arrested a young teenager. They had found him in front of yet another house late last evening in the act of exposing himself. He was not from the neighborhood and apparently he looked a little like me. The police said he confessed to other similar incidents. They had been looking for him for the past few weeks.

It was such a relief to be exonerated but it really did not change much for me. My parents attempted to set the record straight and informed our immediate neighbors I had been cleared of any wrongdoing. For some strange reason they had made up their minds about my guilt and were not listening. Their collective judgment of me did not make any sense.

My babysitting job was gone and I never got the opportunity to say goodbye to those two wonderful little girls. I was treated like a pariah. My reputation was ruined.

The happiest day of my life occurred a year later when my parents announced we were moving to a new neighborhood about four miles away.

Unfortunately, I had learned a sad lesson. There is no guarantee life will be fair and sometimes a person can be punished for something they did not do.

❖ ❖ ❖

Every summer until I was 16 years old I would travel back to the farm just outside Chatham for a month or so. Along with my cousins, I would work from dawn to dusk hoeing, weeding, picking cucumbers and tomatoes. I milked the cows, fed the pigs their slop and collected the chicken eggs. I loved being out-doors and around the animals. It felt good to help my grandparents.

My grandpa taught me about farming. I called him Pepe. He told me about the need for crop rotation. I learned that growing corn really exhausts the soil, so we have to 'rest' the field by planting soy beans every other year. Apparently the beans are like natural fertil-izers because they're able to take nitrogen from the air and put it into the dirt. I'll never forget the beauti-ful soil on his farm. It would crumble in my fingers like brown sugar and it smelled so good. Pepe really knew what he was doing.

He also taught me how to predict the weather by looking at sunrises and sunsets and watching how the leaves in the trees fluttered. Watching the behavior of birds and whether chimney smoke went straight up or sideways provided more clues.

As an added bonus, there were butterflies every-where on the farm and I always packed my net in case a rare specimen appeared.

By now I was really nuts about golf and I brought my clubs and a few balls to the farm as well. With what little free time I had, I would go to the cow pasture and practice. I created a little course that was complete with corn stalks for targets and cow pies as hazards.

My farm experience really cemented the deep respect and reverence I have for the soil and the earth in general. I know where our food comes from. It takes a lot of hard work, a great deal of intelligence and some luck to keep a farm healthy.

I also have to tell you about going to bed each night. I was assigned to a room on the second floor of the farmhouse. It had been used many years before by my mom and her sisters. The room was like something you would see in a museum and it appeared untouched. The closet and dressers were bursting with their old clothes. Since I was all alone, I put on some of the prettier outfits that fit me. I also slept in a nightgown for the first time every night.

On multiple levels, the farm was a magical place for me and I always hated to leave.

❖ ❖ ❖

During my entire time at Cathedral Boys High School, I never dated or went to school socials or dances. I did not even attend my graduation prom. I was certainly attracted to girls and several made it clear they were interested in me. I dreamed of going to movies and hanging out and holding hands and I especially dreamed of kissing a girl.

On looking back I am not sure what was holding me back. I remember stumbling over my words and feeling awkward when I talked to a girl. I considered myself too skinny and I had a big nose and could not imagine anyone finding me attractive. I also think I was fearful of having a girlfriend because inevitably they would want to come to my home. I did not want to take a chance and have them meet my father, especially if he had been drinking. In fact, none of my friends, including Virgilio, ever came over. Some homes in the neighborhood were gathering places and our home was definitely not one of them.

After some reflection, I think the above excuses for not dating are pretty lame. To be completely honest, something else was going on. I think I felt reluctant to get involved with anyone, especially a girl, because inevitably I would have to start talking about my secret. I did not want anyone to know I hated my genitals and always tucked them between my legs to make them 'disappear'. I certainly didn't want anyone to find out I peed sitting down because it's what a girl does. I was not ready to talk about being Bobbi and risk rejection.

I know I appeared to be normal on the outside but I had been told there was something really wrong with me on the inside and I bought into this assessment. I ended up hiding and keeping people at a distance. In effect, I self-imposed a life sentence of solitary confinement for the 'crime' of being me.

Sometimes I wondered if my parents were curious as to why I never went out even though I was 18 years old. If they were, they never said anything. Maybe they secretly thought I was gay?

Now that I have brought it up, I want to make it clear I never felt attracted to guys in any kind of romantic or sexual way. I am not telling you this as a point of pride. It is just a statement of fact.

❖ ❖ ❖

I graduated from high school and was proud of my scholastic and athletic achievements. I was awarded an academic scholarship to McMaster University. It's one of the oldest and most prestigious institutions in Canada and I chose the honors biology program. My interest in entomology was still intense.

Like most of my peers, I had a summer job to cover the expenses of books, food, transportation and lab equipment. I found work at the Hamilton Department of Streets and Sanitation. I did various jobs including garbage truck detail, painting guardrails and cutting weeds with a scythe in public parks. Using a jackhammer all day in the summer heat was intensely physical work.

I became very well acquainted with flies and maggots on the garbage truck. The pay was excellent and being in the company of regular, working class men was enjoyable. I learned how tough it was to make a dollar and respected how hard they worked. They took great pride in being expert at their particular job.

During my first week at work, I was assigned to a crew that was installing some fencing. I was ordered by the foreman to go to the supply shop and get a box of 'post-holes' for the job. Without thinking I walked over to the supply store and asked the manager for some post-holes which, upon further reflection, do not really exist. He laughed and laughed at me. Word quickly spread through the entire work crew how stupid this new college boy really was. They never let me off the hook about that incident.

I drove my balloon tire bicycle to that job every day. I had my driver's license but I did not have access to the family car very often and needed more practice behind the wheel. I repeatedly begged one of the foremen to give me lessons during our lunch breaks.

You're probably wondering why I'd become obsessed with driving all of a sudden. Well there was a good chance I was going on my first date soon and I wanted to look competent and cool. You heard me correctly. I, Robert Douglas Lancaster, was going on a date and her name was Sarah. I know you are anxious to hear about the details but first I have some driving to do. I can't pick her up on my bicycle.

One day while on lunch break, the foreman handed me some keys and pointed to an enormous water truck in the yard. "You can go drive that truck around the yard and practice driving. Don't hit anything," he said. It had a standard transmission and I had never used a clutch before. The truck was loaded with over 2000 gallons of water.

I climbed up to the driver's seat and started the engine. By now most of the workers had filed out of the lunchroom and were in the yard to watch the proceedings. They knew what was about to happen. The whole thing was a set up. I stalled the truck repeatedly when I let out the clutch. Finally I really revved the engine and released the clutch and the truck leaped forward. I was startled and jammed on the brakes. The engine stalled. This got the water violently sloshing in the huge tank behind the cab. It would rush to the front with great force and the truck would literally jump forward off of the ground. Then the water would slosh backward and the truck would jump to the rear a few feet. It was like I was riding a gigantic bucking bronco. This cycle repeated itself over and over until the water stopped sloshing. All of the crew were killing themselves laughing. They had seen this 'show' many times before with other student workers.

I was certainly book smart and a little farm smart too. But when it came to being street smart, I had a lot to learn. Over the next few summers, I became very good friends with these workers. Many would become patients of mine in just a few short years. However I am getting ahead of myself.

I did date Sarah during the summer and fall of 1969. She was the sister-in-law of one of my best golf buddies. Ben was a little older than me and he was a great golfer. He played at the public golf course called Chedoke in

Hamilton and he worked shifts at the giant steel mill in town. I was a member at Chedoke too and was, in fact, the Club champion even though I had just turned nineteen. He admired my game and caddied for me in several Ontario provincial championships. I had met his wife Susie on a few occasions and she was originally from Nova Scotia.

Apparently her sister, Sarah, had left home and was staying with them. Ben thought it would be fun to introduce her to me. He told me that she and I were the same age and she was bored and lonely. I agreed to a blind date and it was decided we would all go the Canadian National Exhibition in Toronto. I met them at their apartment in Burlington, Ontario and Sarah and I were introduced.

She was almost my height with brown, straight shoulder length hair and she was stunningly beautiful. I was completely taken aback because I had never seen a girl this attractive before. She was very poised and mature and she wore the sexiest summer dress with slits on either side that exposed her tiny waist.

I was completely intimidated and out of my league. I sat in the back seat with her on the way to Toronto and we made small talk.

We all enjoyed the day in spite of the fact I became sick on one of the roller coasters. Sarah and I agreed to meet again. Ben would loan me his car and I took her to the movies. One film we saw was 'Goodbye

Columbus' starring Ali MacGraw. I held her hand for the first time. Hers was very warm and mine was cold and dripping with perspiration. We also went to restaurants and a concert at McMaster featuring The Turtles and the Chicago Transit Authority. I taught her how to play golf and I even brought her home to meet my mom and dad. We exchanged birthday and Christmas presents.

This could have been the time of my life but I was too nervous and self-conscious to enjoy it. I never really felt comfortable around her and would run out of things to say. I never attempted to kiss her and I had the distinct impression she was just tolerating me and hoping to meet someone more interesting. I was basically clueless and had no idea what I was doing.

Sarah gradually failed to return phone calls and finally things ended before any relationship had even started. I found out she was dating a guy who owned a Camaro and she eventually married him. If I were her, knowing how messed up I was inside, I would have dumped me too. But it still hurt and I cried for a long time. In fact, I am tearful right now thinking about the breakup even though it took place almost fifty years ago. Have I ever told you how much I hate Camaros?

Later I'll tell you more about Sarah, but for now I want to return to my life as a biology student. I had to get over my summer love, refocus and concentrate on my studies.

During the second semester of my freshman year, I met a biology classmate called Mary Jo. She was very pretty in a Doris Day kind of way and she was dating an old Cathedral Boys classmate of mine by the name of Mike. We became lab partners.

I completed the year with a somewhat less than stellar academic ranking. It was the first time in my life I did not have straight A's in all my subjects. I found the transition from high school to university very challenging and my parents were not able to help me. They had never attended university. In fact none of my relatives had ever gone to college before. It took a while to get organized and find my place. The year had not been a total loss because I had secured a spot on the Varsity Golf Team.

Now it was time to enjoy the summer break before my sophomore year. Once again, I was hired as a laborer for Streets and Sanitation.

During that summer of 1970, I competed in several major golf championships. Even though I had very little time to practice given my summer job, I played quite well.

I daydreamed of becoming a professional golfer. In fact that dream took root after I went to my first Canadian

Open with my dad to watch Arnold Palmer play. I was 15 years old at the time and very impressionable. It looked like a glamorous life that involved money, travel, interviews, autograph requests and fame.

I had no idea what steps were needed to elevate my game to a professional level. I never had a coach and did not have a mentor. At Chedoke I was surrounded by much older, opinionated players who would remind me I didn't have what it took. Their most frequent comment was, "You're not tough enough. You're too nice."

I wasn't quite sure what they meant about being too nice. Maybe they were right though, because when I competed at the highest level, a recurring theme emerged. I would have runs of really stellar play and would find myself in the lead or close to it. But inevitably self-doubt would creep in and I would falter when the pressure was most intense. I did not have any strategies to deal with the situation and I would slip back in to the pack.

I want to tell you about a life-changing event that occurred early that summer of 1970. It took place during a tournament on a smaller stage where I was quite confident and dominant.

I was playing in the final round of the Chedoke Club Championship. I had a huge lead and was on the tee of the next to last hole. I looked to my right at the gallery and to my surprise Mary Jo, my lab partner, was standing in the shade of a large maple tree! She had come to the event with her brother Greg to follow me. What was she doing here? I was confused and more than a little distracted. I won the event and then we chatted after the round. In fact we talked a long time and the next thing I knew, we were dating.

It was so comfortable to be with her. I felt relaxed and talked for hours about golf, butterflies, hummingbirds, the farm, the piano, and everything in between. She learned about my humble roots and my father's alcoholism. She just accepted the entire mess and we became inseparable.

And yes, I kissed her and did everything imaginable with her. I still sat and peed like a girl and I wore lingerie sometimes but otherwise, I had become a bad boy and my hormones were surging. I still did not like my genitals but at least I was finally putting them to good use.

Now where were those nuns from my youth who scolded me for kissing an eight year old classmate on the cheek? Perhaps they were busy handing a doll to some other young boy to teach him a lesson.

Mary Jo's parents were very wealthy and I became part of their social circle. I went with them to restaurants that were beyond anything I had ever experienced. They gave us theatre tickets and we enjoyed plays and musicals like The King and I, My Fair Lady, Show Boat and Oklahoma. These productions were incredible but they were nothing compared to the torrid love story that was unfolding starring Bob and Mary Jo. I would have been in serious trouble if her parents had found out how much I was corrupting their precious young Catholic daughter.

We began our sophomore year together and I was full of myself. I became a straight-A-student again and captained the varsity golf team to the first of two Ontario University Athletic Association championships. I was now living in an apartment just off campus. Mary Jo embraced the female part of me. She did not seem to care as long as no one else found out. She made me female clothes and bought me shoes and a wig. She loved me and that meant all of me and this was just part of the package.

I taught her how to play golf and she and her other brother Mike taught me how to play tennis. Our favorite song was 'Close To You' by the Carpenters.

When I was alone at my apartment, I would dress entirely as Bobbi. I was reluctant to have Mary Jo see me transformed completely because I feared something might finally click and she would be turned off and leave me. I ventured out occasionally but I was absolutely petrified of being found out. Most of the time, I played it safe and hid like I'd always done.

Mary Jo and I continued to be best friends, lab partners and lovers and in the blink of an eye we were engaged to be married. My parents had moved to Ottawa with Ron, Sandy and Ken. Dad had found an even better job opportunity in the nations' capitol. His drinking continued and I feared for my mom because I was not there to protect her anymore.

Sure enough, I got a call from her one evening in the summer of 1972. Mom was in a motel room with Ken and Sandy. She had argued with Dad about some insignificant thing. He was particularly drunk and beat her. Apparently he threatened to kill her, Sandy and Ken. Mom had escaped with them to a motel and she called me for help.

I borrowed Mary Jo's Toyota Corolla for the long five hour drive and arrived at the motel just as the sun was coming up. Mom was so frightened. Her face was very swollen and bruised. Sandy and Ken were silent and wooden.

"Mom, I am so very sorry. Do you want to go to the hospital?"

"No."

"Do you want me to call the police?"

She shook her head.

With that said, I told her I was going to find Dad and have it out with him. I was going to make certain this never happened again.

"Wait for me here and I'll be back soon," I said. She nodded and sat down in a chair, exhausted.

I left the motel and went to look for my father. I was a slim and athletic ball of rage and ready to explode. I found him in a hotel room near his office in downtown Ottawa. He was an unshaven, smelly, disgusting forty-five year old mess. I shoved him around and knocked him over. I begged him to take a swing at me because I wanted to hit him back hard. He knew better and became passive. Five of him could not have controlled me. As I pinned him against the wall with my fist cocked, I growled at him through clenched teeth that if he ever laid a finger on my mom again, I would kill him. He knew I meant it. At that moment, I had become an out-of-control animal and I hope to never experience that sensation again in my life. I threw him aside and stomped out of his room.

I returned to Mom and told her she could safely go back home because after my talk with Dad she had nothing to fear. I stayed for three more days. He returned home too and offered his well-worn apologies and promises. The situation was awkward as heck. Then I returned to Hamilton and my future life with Mary Jo.

My marriage in December of that year was fast approaching and about a month before the event, I got a call from my father. We had not talked since that awful day, which was just fine with me.

He had decided on a wedding gift and wanted to tell me about it. "Bob, my wedding gift for you is quite simple. I will never drink again and that is a promise. It will help me be a better person and I hope it will help win you back." I responded sarcastically, "How wonderful" and hung up.

Our great, big, fabulous wedding was the social event of the year. My mom and dad looked great. And, you know something? Dad never did touch another drop of alcohol again. He did not go to therapy or AA or anything else. He just 'white knuckled it,' I guess.

Mary Jo and I finished our studies. She became a nurse. I abandoned my butterflies and decided to help people instead. I was accepted into medical school at McMaster in 1972 and now I was dreaming of being a family physician.

My studies went well until my final year, called the Clinical Clerkship. During that period of training, it is expected you will assume more responsibility for patients, present cases at grand rounds and participate in on-call nights as well. My duties also included teaching and providing guidance for younger medical students. The pressure gets ratcheted up as does the scrutiny of one's performance.

Early in this Clerkship year, I did something that stunned everyone. I quit medical school. My parents were dumbfounded and my in-laws were aghast. I told everyone I really wanted to pursue other career options, but my plans were vague.

Dr. Ron McAuley was one of my professors and advisors. He was a Family Doctor and had taken a liking to me. He prevented me from resigning and arranged for a leave of absence instead. He kept in touch every few months to see how I was doing. Dr. McAuley did not explore why I quit. He just assumed I needed a time out.

Another professor called to tell me I should be ashamed of myself. I had wasted tax dollars and had robbed some other student of a place in the class. He called me a selfish person who did not appreciate the opportunity I was throwing away. He was incensed and did not mince words. It was painful to listen to.

I am certain you are wondering why I quit. Like most things in life, it was complicated. First of all, I had this growing sense I was in over my head. I had doubts about my knowledge base. I was fearful of being responsible for patients' lives all by myself in the middle of an on-call night. It was similar to the self-doubt I experienced in major golf championships. I lacked confidence.

Also I did not know of another doctor anywhere who was cross-dressing. Believing I was a flawed and very sinful person, I did not deserve to be a doctor and a moral pillar of the community. My secretive behavior was disqualifying.

My already fragile ego was further damaged when, on several occasions, a professor or department head took me to task in front of the other Clerks and ridiculed my management of a patient. It was like I was standing in front of the school assembly all over again when I was eight and being humiliated with a doll. I took the criticism so personally that it wounded me. The other Clerks received similar treatment and just brushed it off.

All of this self-doubt and angst came to a head one day. As part of our training, all the Clerks had to participate in an exercise. Each one of us had to be video-taped seeing a 'mock' patient. Later our history taking, examination skills, problem solving and management plan would be viewed and critiqued by the class and our professors. I dreaded this clinical test for weeks. One by one I watched my peers participate in the process. Some were polished and professional. Others were under-performing and they received scathing comments. I couldn't imagine being judged by the class and not measuring up.

Finally it was my turn and by that point, I was a mess. I was hyperventilating and my throat closed so I could barely talk. My hands were visibly shaking and my mind went blank. I was sitting in a room with my classmates and was told to proceed to the examination room next door where the programmed patient was waiting for me. Everyone would be able to see me through a one-way mirror and the encounter was being recorded. I refused to leave my seat. The professor insisted and really pressured me to cooperate. I became stiff and resisted the gentle pushing and prodding of my class-mates. Then I stood up abruptly, declared I'm not going to do it and raced from the room. I kept walking faster and faster to get as far away as possible. I quit medical school the next day and offered my lame reasons for resigning.

I was obviously in need of a father, a mentor, a thera-pist or all the above. I did not understand my behavior or the underlying issues driving it.

On looking back, I now realize the doll incident and other similar public shamings during my formative years had traumatized me. It had led to an intense fear of being in front of an audience. Once 'triggered', I would resort to a fight-or-flight mentality and usually I would flee. This condition is now called PTSD.

Deep down, I hated myself for quitting and really missed my books and classmates. I became depressed and kept all of this to myself because I was too proud to ask for help. In my mind, the need for counseling was a sign of weakness. I also feared a psychiatrist would likely uncover my secret.

Mary Jo was mystified as to why I quit. However she did not ask many questions and simply loved and supported me. She kept telling her very worried parents I needed a break and urged them to be patient.

Of course we needed money so I had to find work. I drove for Yellow Cab. The dispatcher became aware of my medical training and witnessed my compassion and patience with challenging customers. He arranged for me to transport disabled children to school and old people to and from senior centers and doctor appointments.

I also worked in the pro shop at Chedoke golf course and sold men's clothing at a department store. All the while I thought about being Bobbi and how much I still wanted to help people as a physician. I was a lost soul.

The months clicked by. After more than two years of wandering in the desert of my life, I woke up one morning and was sick of the taxi business. I was fed up with my directionless existence. I was tired of feeling broken. Enough was enough.

I looked at myself in the mirror and told myself I was not a loser. I felt strongly that my destiny was to be a doctor. It felt like the right time to resume my correct path. I was older, more mature and somewhat beat up. I also had come to realize that physicians were not perfect people and it was unrealistic to hold myself to some impossible standard.

I had a powerful feeling that it was not about me anymore; it was about helping others.

By returning to school I would have to face confrontational professors and all my self-doubts. Deep inside, I felt up to the challenge.

I told Mary Jo I was going back and of course she was thrilled. My next call was to Dr. McAuley who rejoiced at the news. However he was concerned because my leave of absence had expired and there appeared to be no protocol available to reinstate me. He went to the Dean and the admissions committee and lobbied on my behalf. Ultimately, I was allowed back in.

I returned to my studies with fierce determination and a confidence that surprised me. I was not going to let Dr. McAuley down. I was closely watched for any signs of a meltdown but displayed nothing for anyone to be worried about. There were many times when I was required to be front and center and my emotions were 'triggered'. However my fight-or-flight button seemed to be permanently switched to the fight position now. I would push back and defend my positions like never before.

I went on to complete my internship and during my residency was voted Chief Resident. This was a great honor and I felt enormously respected and very proud. Eventually I opened a private practice and my roster of patients included some of my professors and their families. It also included nurses, physical and occupational therapists, social workers, colleagues, Streets and Sanitation workers, golf professionals, neighbors, friends of friends and everyone else in between. I was popular and worked hard to maintain everyone's respect.

None of the care I provided for tens of thousands of patients would ever have happened without Dr. Ron McAuley. He truly believed in me and my ability to help people and I hope he is resting in peace.

Initially Mary Jo and I enjoyed an incredibly happy marriage but we encountered sorrow as well. We experienced infertility. Time after time, Mary Jo would miscarry early in pregnancy. Ultimately we adopted our first child, then had one of our own and finally adopted a third special needs child. We became very busy to say the least. She stayed at home with the children. The third child's medical complications in particular placed an enormous burden upon her.

At the same time, I was busy ministering to my patients. I was delivering hundreds of babies, assisting at surgeries, caring for hospitalized patients and making house calls. I volunteered in the community and was on too many hospital committees.

We were basically engaged in parallel lives and there was no Bob and Mary Jo time anymore. We were in trouble as a couple but we didn't know it yet.

Dr. Bob 1984

As if all this wasn't enough, I had no time to be Bobbi. However, I thought about her every day. The yearning to just be the woman I knew myself to be was constant.

I debated not telling you about the following because it is going to make me appear crazy. However, I think it's important for you to experience the desperation I felt. If you are squeamish, you might want to skip this next part.

I had read about people like me who had some medical training and who had surgically removed their own genitals. I know it sounds gross and almost unbelievable. I must admit there was a time when I contemplated performing this surgery on myself using local anesthesia. The fact of the matter was my surgical skills were not great and I don't think I could have contorted myself enough to see what I was doing. I was never very flexible. Also I feared experiencing excessive bleeding or pain and passing out. Then I'd really be in trouble.

I warned you this admission would sound like crazy thinking and it probably was. However, I need you to appreciate how absolutely intolerable it is to live in a body that does not match the brain's sense of self and the lengths some people will go to make it right.

Here is another thing you should be aware of. I have already explained how I enjoyed dressing like a woman. Aside from that I had a deep seated desire to function like one.

For example, there were times I wanted to be pregnant and watch my body change as a new life developed inside me. I wanted to experience labor and fight and scream to give life to my baby. I dreamed of breast feeding and nurturing my own child.

Of course I knew this was impossible. However it didn't stop me from thinking about it. Many others like me have confessed to similar yearnings. These pregnancy desires were more intense when I was younger. I can't remember when I stopped dreaming about having a child because it was such a long time ago.

Since I was powerless to change the unchangeable, I had to soldier on and accept my situation. I took comfort in helping others. Patients depended on me. I witnessed first and last breaths. My work as a physician was beyond special and it allowed me to focus on something other than myself.

❖ ❖ ❖

It was early in my professional career when a couple of incidents occurred that you should know about. They foreshadow the human rights advocacy I now participate in.

The first involved the Ontario Medical Association. Like every young doctor, I joined this professional organization when I opened the doors of my practice. The OMA united physicians in a powerful way. It interacted with the provincial government and advocated for improvements in health care delivery. It also lobbied to secure a more favorable fee schedule.

In general, doctors were very unhappy about their shrinking incomes. Negotiations became polarized and an impasse was reached. The OMA finally threatened the government with a strike involving all the doctors in Ontario if their demands for more pay were not met.

The OMA called a general meeting in Toronto and thousands of physicians convened to vote on the strike action. Basically if a strike occurred, only emergency services would be available for patients. It meant I would personally have to close my office door.

In effect, I was being told to abandon my practice. I could not bear the thought of turning my back on my pregnant patients who were due to deliver at any moment. I had promised to be at their deliveries. We had bonded over the course of their prenatal visits. They had attended natural childbirth classes and had engaged a lactation consultant upon my recommendation. They knew I was going to help them through their childbirth because I was not a doctor who showed up at the last minute. I was going to be their labor coach because that's what I did.

There was no way the OMA was going to keep me from these obstetrical patients at one of the biggest moments of their lives because of a dispute over fee schedules. Not to mention the rest of my practice. What about my dying patients and their families, the ones I was visiting at their homes? What would I say to them? "Sorry, I am on strike and I can't visit you today."

When I started my practice, I made an unwritten contract with every one of my patients to always be there for them. If I was away, I would make certain my on-call group was available and ready to step in. It would take a much more important issue than money to force me to close my door.

I raised my hand at that rancorous OMA meeting and voted NO.

I was one of a handful of doctors who also voted no. Of course the strike still took place. It lasted about a week but I went to work every day and my patients really appreciated my commitment to them.

During that week, my phone lines were sabotaged. I was threatened by colleagues and was called a scab. The provincial government did not budge and the public turned against the 'money-grabbing' doctors. The OMA finally called a halt and everyone returned to work. It took a very long time for relationships to be repaired, but at least I had courageously stood up for my principles. I had learned something about myself in the process and I resigned from the association.

The second incident pitted me against the establishment. Mr. and Mrs. Benvenuto were longtime patients of mine. I had delivered their children and we had a very solid relationship.

One night at about 1:00 AM, my home phone rang. It was Mr. Benvenuto. He told me the fourteen year-old daughter of their best friends was in hospital and she was close to death. This family, like the Benvenuto's, were Jehovah's Witnesses and the daughter was in need of a blood transfusion to save her life. Her parents were refusing the treatment. Their doctor had removed himself from her care because the parents were not cooperating. Mr. Benvenuto was hoping I would meet with the parents to see if I could serve as their daughter's attending physician.

He also stressed the immediacy of the situation. Lawyers were arriving at the hospital and there was going to be an emergency hearing in front of a judge at 3:00 A.M. In summary, the province was petitioning to have the fourteen year old removed from her parents' authority and become a ward of the province so the doctors could proceed with the transfusions.

I could have said no to Mr. Benvenuto but something deep inside compelled me to go and at least assess the situation. The Jehovah Witness community was a minority and they were frequent targets of the establishment because they believed in a different ideology. I arrived at the hospital at 2:00 A.M., introduced myself to the parents and briefly looked at the chart. There was an incredibly hostile atmosphere permeating the entire ward.

Apparently the fourteen year old had been experiencing a routine menstrual cycle when the bleeding became heavier. Over the next several days the menstrual flow turned into a torrent and the patient lost consciousness. She was admitted to the intensive care unit. Intravenous hormone therapy, fluids and oxygen were given and the bleeding ceased.

I think it stopped because she was almost out of blood. I remember her hemoglobin was 2.8 and this level is almost incompatible with life. It was at that point the doctors really pushed her parents to accept the transfusions. Of course they reminded the doctors their religion forbids receiving blood products of any kind.

I walked down the hall to the patient's room. It looked like I was entering a morgue. She was as white as the sheets and her heart beat was rapid and weak. The bed was in a slightly head down position. I introduced myself. She answered my questions with an almost inaudible voice. I had to literally place my head against her head so I could hear her.

I asked, "Do you realize you are dying?"

"Yes."

"Are you scared?"

"No." She added, "If I die, I will go to heaven and everything will be all right."

"Is your religion important to you or just to your parents?"

"My religion means everything to me. It is the best thing about my life."

I was taken aback by her sincerity and her conviction. I told her the hospital doctors wanted to give her blood transfusions and I asked how she felt about that. She became very agitated. She stated, "I will fight them to my death. I will tear the IV from my arm."

She was really upset and her pulse rate and breathing became dangerously fast. I thought she was going to arrest right in front of me. I tried to settle her down and I told her I would be there to care for her and defend her. She gradually calmed.

I left the room and proceeded to the judicial hearing that was just getting started. It was in a class room to the right of the nurses' station. I had never attended anything like this before. I was sworn in and realized I was the only doctor representing the patient and her parents. The opposing side was complete with some of the finest gynecologists, hematologists and endocrinologists in the city. They all had been my teachers.

Finally it was my turn to testify and the judge listened very carefully while I informed him of how important the young patients' beliefs were to her. I also told him any attempt to start a transfusion would rapidly lead to her death because she would resist and fight to her last breath. I made it clear that even now, she was as close to death as a person could be.

The judge adjourned for about fifteen minutes. When he returned he ruled in favor of the family and the room emptied very rapidly. There were nasty looks aimed at me. There was no time to celebrate. I now had the onerous responsibility of serving as the girl's only doctor.

To be honest, I was scared. I called several very dear colleagues who gave me information on how to hormonally stabilize her uterus and how to enhance her bone marrow's ability to make more blood. They gave me great advice but they did not want to be officially involved.

I continued the IV fluids and visited several times a day. I nurtured and encouraged her in every possible way. Ever so slowly she gained strength and in a little over a week, my patient was able to walk out of hospital. I still can't believe she survived.

Once again, I was at odds with some of the physicians in the community. They refused to accept my referrals or phone calls after the incident. However, I did not let that bother me. I felt proud of the fact I had respected and defended another individual's firmly held religious beliefs. She was prepared to die before she would abandon her principles and I stood right there with her.

Furthermore, I learned that ordering the medically correct therapy could, at times, be the absolutely wrong thing to do if you did not approach a patient holistically.

So there you have it. I think these two incidents allow you to get to know where my head and my heart live. The events are etched in my memory. They were fundamental in helping me discover who I really am as a person.

Immediately after, I finished my charting and order-writing and left the ward at about 5:00 A.M. I had been up all night and was about to face a very busy office in just three hours. I had parked in the underground lot beneath the hospital and, after I flashed my parking pass and exited the structure, I immediately found myself stopped by a red light on Main Street. I sat and thought about the events of the last few hours. Within a few blocks I was stopped by yet another red light.

At that instant, from out of nowhere, I was jolted by a sudden moment of clarity. I did not hear a voice, but had a revelation and the message was blunt: I was never going to live my life as Bobbi. There was no way forward. My fate was sealed.

I experienced an immediate sadness and hopelessness that was overwhelming. I started to cry and it progressed to uncontrollable sobbing. This unfiltered emotion emanated from somewhere deep inside and I had to pull off to the side of the road. It took fifteen minutes to regain my composure.

Finally I rejoined what was by now rush hour traffic and was stopped by several more signals. I just wanted to run the red lights and get home.

This was the first time I had experienced such distress and it would not be the last. As time passed, I discovered whenever I had a quiet moment or two I would be seized by an unbearable sadness. I could not see any path that would allow Bobbi to emerge. I was going to be relegated to a life of longing and hiding. Tears of despair would flow immediately and the pain was unbearable.

My life had become a never-ending red light.

The only solution was to stay busy and engaged all the time. That meant figuratively avoiding stop lights because they only afforded me a few minutes to think and fall apart. I cranked up the treadmill of never ending duties to the fastest possible setting and carried on.

This was no way to live.

❖ ❖ ❖

My parents moved back to Hamilton in 1982 where they bought an old home across the street from McMaster Medical Center. I think Dad was depressed and burned out and he had taken an early retirement.

Mom had completed her high school studies while they were in Ottawa and I was proud of her. In spite of my father's constant reminders that she was stupid and incompetent, Mom secured a great job at the university. It was finally her time to shine.

Dad was still sober after all those years but he was a damaged human being. None of us saw this coming but in the summer of 1984, he died suddenly in his sleep at the age of 57. Not a tear was shed at the time.

Finality is word I don't use a lot but this was finality. I would never have the opportunity to say goodbye to my father or apologize for threatening to kill him. There would be no chance to repair our relationship ever again. Nevertheless, that did not stop me from trying.

I'll tell you more about that later.

❖ ❖ ❖

Time passed quickly and I was tired of fighting with the Ontario government-run health system in order to obtain care for my patients. I had also made some very bad financial decisions involving an investment advisor. Bankruptcy was looming and we were going to lose our house. My relationship with Mary Jo had become an empty shell. Her life revolved around the children and my life revolved around my patients.

We talked and decided that, since we were floundering anyway, why not shake things up and start anew. Many of our doctor friends were moving to Arizona where they enjoyed better professional opportunities. There were several superior private schools just waiting for our children. The weather was much better too. In spite of the objections of my mom and her parents, Mary Jo and I immigrated to Phoenix in 1991 for a better life and a fresh start.

It did not take long for things to fall apart. But the purpose of this book is not to document the final stages of a struggling relationship. I am not about to tell the world the very personal things that contributed to our unraveling. However I will tell you that Mary Jo and our kids are still alive and well and I love them very much.

I am going to make a broad observation about my first marriage as it relates to my gender identity struggles. Our relationship worked initially because, amazingly, Mary Jo had no difficulty seeing me dressed as a woman as long as no one else found out, especially the kids. However when it came to me actually taking on some of the more stereotypical female tasks, it became clear, albeit unspoken, I was to stay in a traditional male lane. She expected me to work hard like the other men in her family, which meant I would be the breadwinner and be gone all day. I was also expected to be the disciplinarian when I got home and do the usual manly outdoor chores.

Mary Jo had my dream job. She stayed home and raised the children and performed the multiple homemaking duties. Her tasks were no easier than mine. However I longed to be home as well.

We had, by all appearances, a successful, traditional kind of marriage. The difficulty was that I wasn't typical. Maybe I should have pushed back and not quietly accepted the status quo. But how hard should I have pushed? Mary Jo had accepted my cross-dressing when most women I know would have run for the door. I decided to put my head down and accept my good fortune and soldier on.

In the end, our marriage failed for multiple complicated reasons. It was beyond sad.

I was walking amidst the embers of my first marriage when I met Lucy. It was the summer of 1995 and she was assigned to help care for patients in my very busy, hospital-run family practice. We were in the trenches together managing some extremely challenging patients. We observed each other under the most trying of circumstances and had the opportunity to discuss every imaginable topic on a daily basis.

Toward the end of 1996, we both felt we might have a personal future together. However there was a huge issue I had not broached and I had to find a way to introduce my female side to the relationship. I was not brave enough to bring it up directly.

One evening, I dressed in some obviously female undergarments and attended a black tie party with her. She hugged me and felt a bra under my tuxedo. Lucy was initially surprised but she never lost her composure. As a former critical care and ICU nurse, she was unflappable.

In fact she initially found my cross-dressing to be novel and somewhat kinky and over time, I tried to introduce it more and more. This proved uncomfortable for her and one day she made it very clear she didn't want to see me dressed as a woman anymore.

Aside from the cross-dressing, she was thrilled I was not a typical guy. For example, she would tell me I was a great doctor but an even better nurse and she meant it as a compliment. You see, Lucy had observed me in action with people. She was touched by my gentleness and compassion. She noted I spent time with my patients and touched them and assisted with typical nurse-related concerns.

She was also thrilled that I liked to dust and clean the house and bragged about my interior decorating skills.

She was in awe of my piano playing, flower arranging and gardening talents. Lucy was also amazed how dogs, cats, birds and nature in general would bond with me so easily. She loved all of the complex parts of my personality. It appeared she was really attracted to all the stereotypical female parts of me.

My relationship with Lucy, as it related to my gender identity issues, was the exact opposite of my first marriage.

What I am trying to say is that Mary Jo could accept me dressed as a female but she demanded I adopt a stereotypical male role in our relationship. On the other hand, Lucy was repulsed by seeing me dressed as a woman but embraced my female personality traits and interests.

We ended up committing to each other and were married in 1999. Lucy and I felt like soul mates joined at the heart. Our friends appeared to be envious of our rich relationship. We were a sure thing.

Wedding Day, May 25, 1999, North Fork of Ghost River, Banff

Of course, nothing is a sure thing when one person in the relationship is in trouble.

I was still hiding. I was secretly cross-dressing, sitting to pee, longing to be Bobbi and crying uncontrollably whenever I had a few quiet moments.

My marriage might have been new, but the hiding had become very old. The fast pace of the red light avoiding life I had created had finally exhausted me. I felt trapped and hopeless and was tired of being me. Enough was enough.

Let this be a warning: The next chapter is going to revolve around a very disturbing event in my life. I think we should both take a few deep, slow breaths before I pull down the shades. We are about to enter the blackness.

*"All I want is blackness,
blackness and silence."*

SYLVIA PLATH

Three

Humpty Dumpty

Giving up is something we all eventually have to face. Perhaps acceptance and surrender is a better way to put it. Some of us have our life unexpectedly snatched away in mid-stride because of an accident, a medical catastrophe, an act of hate or just being in the wrong place at the wrong time. When that happens, there is no time to contemplate or to surrender.

However, for most, giving up comes after a prolonged decline. We finally run out of the will to struggle against the cancer or heart failure or whatever final burden we are carrying. And then we pass away.

I am here to tell you I gave up. There were so many seeds of surrender that I allowed to take root. I'm not sure which issue played the bigger role. Possibly it was the bankruptcy and subsequent financial struggle. Perhaps it was the failure of my first marriage and the breaking of my promise, "until death do us part." Maybe it was the knowing I was responsible for the pain unleashed on our children as a result of the divorce. Or possibly it was the pressure of caring for so many patients for such a long time in an ever more insane healthcare system that finally caused me to break.

In looking back, I think the most important thing that led to my surrender was a lifetime of hiding. The longing to just live a true and authentic life as the woman I knew I was became unbearable. I felt trapped. The prospect of finally coming out of the closet was bleak. The situation was hopeless. Anytime I found myself alone, I would just start crying.

So I gave up. It felt like all the air had been released from my body. I did not feel like trying anymore and there was not a butterfly or a hummingbird in sight to lift my spirits.

I began the organized plan that would lead to my self-destruction. I chose the method carefully, picked the date and spent several weeks writing the most gut-wrenching letters to Lucy, my children, Mom, my siblings and Mary Jo. I explained to each and every one of them why I had to leave and I apologized. I addressed and stamped all the letters and hid them well in a compartment in my briefcase. They would be mailed very soon.

I was tired of going so fast. It was going to be such a relief to put an end to my suffering. I knew I was going to shock and hurt a lot of people, but I had to look after myself. I was exhausted trying to be Bob when I knew I was Bobbi.

I felt like a big egg that had cracked into a hundred pieces. It had become impossible to hold myself together.

One day I told Lucy I didn't feel well and was going to stay home. This was all part of my final plan. She was thrilled I was looking after myself for a change and not always putting my patients' needs first. She thought I likely had a virus and had no way of knowing my death was only two days away. I spent that first 'sick day' at home tidying up details.

I called in sick the next day as well. Lucy left for work and as soon as she was out of sight, I got in my car and went directly to Papago Golf Course in Phoenix. I wanted to play golf all by myself and enjoy a final round on my last day. I chose Papago because it was a municipal golf course and it reminded me of Chedoke where I'd learned to play the game so many years ago.

I was getting my clubs out of the trunk when a fellow in the parking lot recognized me. Mark walked over to ask if he could play with me. I definitely did not want to play with him or anyone else. But being the ever so polite Canadian to the very end, I agreed he could join me.

This was not our first encounter.

I had met Mark a few years earlier. At the time he was a fellow competitor on the Western States Professional

Golf Tour. He was a handsome, athletic man who was larger than life and looked like a movie star. He owned and operated a hunting company when he wasn't playing professional golf, taking wealthy clients on safaris to Africa. I was his polar opposite, skinny and unassuming. I'd been making plans to qualify for the Senior PGA Tour and had to find out whether I possessed the talent necessary to succeed. As you know, I'd dreamed of being a professional golfer when I was young but had become a doctor instead.

I was competing in my second tournament of the tour at Palm Valley Golf Course just west of Phoenix and had low expectations: I'd not played well in the first tournament and was nervous. To my surprise, my swing held up and I managed to control my shaking. At the end of the two day competition, I had tied for first place with Mark and another professional with the unlikely name of 'Wedgy' Winchester. The winner would be determined by a sudden death playoff.

Ten minutes before the playoff, a very strange thing happened to me. I became completely calm. I had never felt so serene and peaceful in my entire life. I was used to feeling like a bundle of nerves during tournaments. This calm was surreal and completely new territory for me.

Wedgy was eliminated after he bogeyed the first hole. I played like never before, hitting perfect shot after perfect shot and finally secured the victory over

Mark after five holes. I was three under par in the play-off and Mark was not pleased he had lost. I arrived back at the clubhouse and was greeted with applause and congratulatory high fives. I enjoyed a beer and was presented with the prize.

I felt so proud of myself and never wanted that day to end. Of all my victories, it stands out the most. I had overcome my doubts and proven to myself I could hold my own against the very best players. Eventually all the contestants left the facility. The sun went down in a blaze of yellow and red. I found myself alone in the parking lot, clutching my cell phone and looking up at the star-filled sky. I had called everyone important to me and told them about my magical day. There were tears of self-satisfaction running down my cheeks. At the time I had no way of knowing I would never experience anything even close to the joy of that moment for the rest of my golfing life.

Now, in a very short time, at least I was going to experience the calm and peacefulness of that playoff once again. There were just a few more hours to go.

Apparently Mark had never forgotten the playoff either because as soon as I agreed to play with him, he announced that today's round would be a rematch and he was going to get revenge. Now things were going from bad to worse and I really did not want to play a competitive match with this fellow for my final round.

He was intense and appeared determined to beat me. He did not know I was already defeated and basically dead inside. I went through the motions and there were moments when I cried privately and could not see the ball through my tears. The eighteen holes came mercifully to an end and he won. I was finished.

I was in the final lap of my time on earth. As I was parking my car in the garage, Lucy rushed out in a panic. She had assumed I'd been home all day recovering from a virus and was alarmed to find the house empty when she returned from work. While waiting and wondering where I was, she sensed something was really wrong. So Lucy did something she'd never done before. She snooped and found the hidden letters in my briefcase and read the one addressed to her. She became hysterical.

Lucy would not let me out of her sight. At her insistence, we went to our family doctor's office and this was followed immediately by a consultation with a psychiatrist. Pills and counselors and psychologists ensued. Family and friends all pitched in to help.

It took all the king's horses and all the king's men to put this Humpty Dumpty back together again.

I did not work for over a year. It's difficult to resuscitate a person who has given up. My partners took over my medical practice and I would never see my precious patients again. Lucy and I moved to a small town outside of Phoenix called Gold Canyon to simplify our life and cut expenses. I was alive and we were together.

Now I had to face all the things I so desperately wanted to escape. On top of everything else, I'd revealed myself to be a quitter and capable of performing the most selfish of acts.

I was not at all certain I was up to the task of living. But I had to try for Lucy.

*"Man is free at the moment
he wishes to be."*

VOLTAIRE

Four

FREE AT LAST

By 2004, I had been participating in very intense counseling for almost two years and my near suicide was in the past. I was given homework to do between therapy sessions. There were assigned books for me to read and notes to take. The conversations revolved around my divorce, the children, my guilt and professional burnout. I was diagnosed with severe clinical depression with suicidal ideation and was told I would need antidepressants for the rest of my life. It was concluded I would never be able to practice medicine again because the stress would likely tip me over the edge.

During that time I filled my days volunteering at the Phoenix Zoo, Phoenix Art Museum and Boyce Thompson Arboretum. I also started a pet-sitting company. They were all interesting, happy and fulfilling activities.

I also started to play golf again with my new golf buddies, Ken, Abe and Roy. They all knew about my depression and the struggle to get back on my feet and were unbelievably supportive. They enjoyed introducing me to cigars and good wine. I was not cut any slack during our matches and was expected to give them lots of strokes in order to negate my superior skills. Being better negotiators, they were winning our golf wagers week after week. However it all worked out because they would buy me lunch with the money I lost to them.

Me at about 50 years old

Even though I was already in my early fifties, I was trying to learn how to be a guy. For better or worse, I had three super-masculine role models to learn from.

Me, Ken, Abe and Roy

❖ ❖ ❖

During one of my last counseling sessions my therapist, Pete, said he was pleased my mood was now stable. He was encouraged I had developed better insight and coping strategies to deal with stress and the inevitable surprises of life. He made certain I was still taking my antidepressants.

At one point he looked up from his notes and said, "You know, Bob, I have to be honest with you. I still sense there is something you are holding back. There is a core of unhappiness about you I just can't figure out, no matter how many questions I ask you." With that said, he stared at me like he was expecting me to solve the mystery.

Of course he was unable to fully understand me because I had witheld information from him. I had never told him about Bobbi. After all the time I'd spent in his Scottsdale office, I had never informed Pete about the most important issue of my life! He did not know about the cross-dressing and my lifelong belief I was a female.

I had guarded this secret as though my life depended on it, not even wanting my therapist to know about my sin. Can you believe how far some people, like me, will go to continue hiding? In the process, I was just short-changing myself.

I never did tell Pete. I thanked him for his help and we shook hands and parted ways.

It was the autumn of 2004 when Lucy and I, along with my son, travelled to Canada to stay with my mom and visit my siblings. We showed Lucy our old home on Scenic Drive and his elementary school. He visited with friends and I played golf with my brother Ken. We had a great time eating and drinking too much.

I had no way of knowing lightning was about to strike. On the final morning of the trip, my mother made pancakes. I was just starting my second helping when everything stopped.

Apparently my son was the first to notice I had stopped eating and slumped forward. The fingers of my left hand were in my glass of orange juice.

He called out to Lucy but she could not arouse me. A chaotic scene ensued and an ambulance was called. I was transported to McMaster Medical Center where I had graduated many years before.

The next thing I remember was being told "Wake up, Dr. Bob. It's time to wake up. Open your eyes." Those words were eerily reminiscent of the time I almost died after my tonsillectomy when I was six years old. I opened my eyes and fully expected to see that same group of nuns dressed in white hovering over me.

I realized I was in an emergency room and it was very bright. It felt like I was waking from a nap. A nurse was fussing with IV tubing nearby when she noticed my eyes were open. In a very loud and excited fashion, she exclaimed, "Dr. Lancaster, you are awake! It's me, Sue Robinson. Remember me? I was your patient back when you practiced in Hamilton and you delivered my two kids."

I did recognize her and remembered she was a terrific nurse. I tried to reply but I couldn't speak correctly. My arm was weak and I was confused. Lucy was there at my side and she told me I had experienced a stroke. This news was unbelievable.

A steady stream of family members began visiting now that I was awake. They were all tearful and behaved as though I was dying. Then to everyone's amazement I improved hour by hour. Tests revealed I had experienced small strokes in multiple areas of my brain and the blockages disappeared quickly without resulting in significant damage. It was still frightening. Once stable, I was discharged from the hospital with a prescription for a blood thinner.

Lucy and I were now anxious to get home because I had no health insurance in Canada. In spite of my mother's dire warnings, we flew back to Phoenix the next day. My balance was still messed up. Specialists determined my neurological event had been caused by a congenital hole in my heart previously unknown to me. It was repaired and I continued to recover.

For me, this stroke represented the last straw. My mortality was now obvious for even me to see. I was not allowed to drive for six months. I used the time to organize my life and put my affairs in order. I got rid of clutter and tossed out items I did not use anymore. Filing cabinets were cleaned out. Living wills and medical power of attorney documents were signed and our family trust was reviewed.

There was one enormous issue I had to take care. I finally had to deal with Bobbi and came to the conclusion I was finished with hiding. I was going to take the steps needed to live a true and authentic life. If that meant that people were going to judge me and reject me, than it would be their loss. They were going to miss out on experiencing the very best of me.

I informed Lucy of my intentions and she very reluctantly watched as I started on my new path. I consulted the best experts in Phoenix. I was diagnosed as a transgender individual and, at long last, participated in open and honest counseling. I felt better than I had in years. I stopped the antidepressants because I knew I was going to be all right. I was full of hope.

Given my renewed energy, I decided to return to my real love, which was caring for people. My previous psychiatrist and counselor had stated emphatically I would never be able to return to the rigors of medical practice. However, I was about to challenge their conclusion.

I was lucky to find work as medical director for two new medical–surgical rehabilitation facilities. I also became a medical director of one of the country's largest non-profit hospice companies.

By all accounts, my work performance was outstanding. I found the hospice work to be the most meaningful professional activity I had ever done. Lucy started to see patients with me at these facilities as well.

I also began a small concierge practice in Gold Canyon and made house calls on these private patients. I was happier than at any other time in my life.

None of my patients, employers or their staff knew about my transgender diagnosis. Of course they noticed

I was allowing my hair to grow to ponytail length. If they looked really closely, they could have seen my breast bumps despite my baggy shirt. Yes, I was on female hormones and my facial hair was disappearing because of painful laser treatments.

I was still hiding because I could not predict their reaction and I did not want to place my employment in jeopardy at this time. However, there was no hiding the changes from Lucy. She loved me very much, but she struggled to understand why I was so obsessed with my gender issues.

Lucy was also looking down the road and could not imagine being married to a woman. She would be considered a lesbian and this did not sit well with her. Lucy hoped that I would come to my senses and just stop this transition. We had many heated discussions, long periods of silence and we cried a lot.

However I was on a mission. Our counselor, Dr. Lewis, tried to support Lucy as much as possible. At the same time, the doctor attempted to slow me down. But I could not be held back because I could 'see the barn'.

In the spring of 2010, my gender-confirmation surgery day finally arrived. There had been a long process leading up to the procedure. I was required to attend counseling and submit to psychological testing. A letter from a psychologist was necessary to confirm the diagnosis of gender identity disorder, now called gender dysphoria. A surgeon will not perform surgery until this process is complete.

I had also received multiple, very painful, electrolysis treatments to my genitals to clear the area of all pubic hair.

My health insurance plan did not cover anything related to my gender dysphoria, including the surgery. The total bill amounted to tens of thousands of dollars.

I drove to the hospital alone the evening before my surgery. Lucy was still not on board. I was not about to stop anything because correcting my brain and body mismatch had become imperative. Without this procedure, I knew I would never be at peace and my very survival was at stake. Anyone can read between those lines.

The pre-operative preparation went smoothly and the next morning, the staff wheeled me in to the operating room. Lucy was nowhere in sight. I felt so alone without my buddy but I had to stay focused. During the next five hours, the surgeon removed my testicles and created female anatomy using my scrotum and parts of my penis. He also performed breast augmentation surgery.

I woke up to catheters, intravenous lines and tubes everywhere. My best friend was still missing.

In spite of experiencing significant pain, I refused narcotics because I feared being impaired and not in control. On a deeper level, I think I wanted to suffer and be punished for the pain I had inflicted on our marriage. Only a person who was raised Catholic would understand this sentiment.

My chest was very swollen and bruised from the breast augmentation surgery. I had a bladder catheter in place. Nevertheless, I had to explore my genital area as gently as I could. Using a mirror, I inspected the bruised, swollen and sutured operative area and my scrotum and penis were gone. At long last they were gone! I finally looked like I should have looked all along. The relief was out of this world.

On the fourth day post-op, Lucy called and said she'd like to visit. She hoped we could find a quiet place to talk. I was thrilled but tried to keep my expectations in check. The staff gave me a pass from the ward for one hour. I still had a bladder catheter in place and the urine bag was secured to my thigh. I warned Lucy I would be dressed as a woman now and my name was Bobbi.

We walked to a restaurant across the street from the hospital. She was smiling and looked happier than I had seen her in months. Something had changed and I was anxious to find out the details of her transformation.

Lucy told me for the past four days she finally had time to think and drink and listen to Don Henley and the Eagles. Don is her favorite singer and songwriter and he speaks to her troubles and to her heart. She has often threatened to leave me for Henley if I give her any more grief. Of course Don would have no say in the matter.

Lucy leaned toward me to tell me how, the night before, she had experienced an epiphany. She described it as an awakening. Her eyes were big and very blue as she provided me with the details. "Bobbi, from out of nowhere, I started to think about the movie actor Christopher Reeve and his wife. Do you remember he starred in the role as Superman and later he was injured in a recreational horseback riding accident? He became quadriplegic and required a ventilator."

I replied, "Yes, I remember that very sad story and I think he died a few years ago. But, what has that got to do with us?"

Lucy continued, "You're right, he did pass away. It's his wife, Dana, who really impressed me. She was at his side for years from the time of his injury until his death. It looked like they were madly in love, just like you and me. She was asked by an interviewer why she stayed with her husband when so many spouses would have left under similar circumstances. I remember her answer. She said that Christopher had obviously changed physically, but the essence of the man she adored was still intact."

I sat back and tried to understand what Lucy was telling me. She continued, "It's just like us! You have changed physically, but all the things about you I fell in love with are still intact. I love your caring, creative, gentle soul and I always will." That was one of the most touching things Lucy had ever said to me and I was speechless.

As if that wasn't enough, she told me about another inspirational couple called the Schechterles. Jason was an on-duty Phoenix police officer in 2001 when his cruiser was struck from behind. His car exploded in flames and he was severely burned. More than fifty surgeries were required and he survived. He was shockingly disfigured and his wife, Suzie, was there with him every painful step of the way.

The Schechterles' marriage not only survived, it thrived. By all accounts his wife had concluded that even though her husband's body had changed, his loving, caring, magnificent personality was still intact. She could not abandon him any more than Mrs. Reeves could have abandoned Christopher. It was the example of these two women that impacted Lucy and revealed the path she would follow. During my post- operative recovery, Lucy re-committed herself to me and our marriage.

She knew people would now assume she was a lesbian. This made her feel uncomfortable but she found a solution. Lucy began to refer to herself as a 'situational' lesbian and that made all the difference in the world for her. I thought the use of the word 'situational' was hysterical and so did our friends.

From that moment on in the restaurant, we knew everything was going to be alright. Just like the Reeves and the Schechterles, Lucy and I have not just survived, we have thrived. We will be together forever.

I have to tell you a beautiful follow-up to this story. A couple of years ago I was given an admission ticket to hear a motivational speaker at the Phoenix Art Museum. The speaker was the one and only Jason Schechterle.

Before his presentation, I saw him standing alone in a sea of three hundred people in the foyer. They were noisily connecting but he was not included. Perhaps his appearance, given his severe scars, was keeping peo-

Hiking in Ontario, 2016

ple at a distance. All I knew was I was not going to allow him to be alone in the crowd for one more second.

I confidently walked up to him, introduced myself and shook his scarred and deformed hand. I proceeded to briefly tell him my story and how his wife had been instrumental in saving my marriage. He was very touched and surprisingly emotional. He said he could not wait to get home and tell her about our meeting. And then we embraced.

There we were. Two physically altered individuals still capable of great things because of the love of our wives.

❖ ❖ ❖

My medical transition was difficult and it was painful. There were some post-op complications. However, the most difficult aspect of all was my social transition. I've already told you about Lucy and me. But there were so many other people involved.

I had to have incredibly emotional conversations with my mom, siblings, adult children, colleagues, patients, golf buddies and friends.

I flew to Canada to talk to my mother face to face because you can only accomplish so much over the phone. I made sure she was sitting down and my sister Sandy was there too, for support. Mom saw me dressed as Bobbi for the first time and she was surprisingly calm. She told me I looked beautiful.

Mom felt very sad because I had carried this burden my entire life and she had not been there to help me.

Mom implied there must have been something lacking in her parenting style.

It has taken repeated conversations to clarify she was not to blame and had nothing to feel guilty about.

At one point, Mom wanted to see my new anatomy. I briefly opened up my bath robe and she and Sandy took a quick peak. They were relieved to discover I appeared so naturally female. They had been expecting terrible scars and disfigurement.

There were emotional discussions with my friends and patients too. Some people understood right away and could not do enough for me and Lucy. Others were shocked and retreated. Let me tell you about a couple of my friends.

I'll start with Roy. He is a golf buddy of mine who I introduced you to earlier in the book. He is also a successful businessman. He's a handsome, large and very strong fellow. He grew up in New Jersey and does not take crap from anyone. Roy is also a Vietnam vet. He is a natural athlete and excelled at sports, especially baseball when he was young.

Unfortunately, a baseball swing best describes his golf swing but he has made up for the deficiencies in his technique with the power of his mind. He is a great competitor and can defeat a superior player because he possesses unbelievable confidence and self-belief.

I know it appears counter-intuitive, but Roy has observed that people in general are fearful of finishing first. They panic and fall apart when winning is within their grasp. He has seen it happen on the golf course and in the boardroom. So he is happy to do the winning. He says he is doing people a favor by removing them from their stress. Roy is thrilled to hold up the trophy and let others feel comfortable with second place.

He also makes cocky statements. He will tell you he likes who he is and always has. He can depend on himself with no questions asked. I enjoy being around Roy and always hope some of his bravado and confident attitude will rub off on me.

Roy was the first friend I talked to about my gender issue. We had just finished playing golf and were enjoying a glass of wine on the club patio. I was very nervous and waited for all the other golfers to leave. Then I started to cry and told him all about me. He listened and said he understood and would help me.

True to his word, he really has helped me in every way. He explained my situation to our golf buddies. He told them I was made this way and really had no other choice except to be myself. He has put people in their place when he heard them making fun of me. He had a party at his house where he reintroduced me to the community. I asked Roy to take me out for dinner so I could practice being out in public as Bobbi and he agreed. He helped make my transition easier.

We have talked endlessly about life, golf, divorces, kids, investments, and everything in between. It has been amazing. The more I openly talked about myself, the more he talked about his own personal disappointments and messes. My relationship with Roy is now more rich and meaningful.

We still meet at his house. He has two large brown leather chairs we settle into. His big screen television is directly in front of us and is always tuned to the Golf Channel but we barely pay attention. We solve the worlds' problems while sipping on Chardonnay.

Roy had never met a transgender person. He did not read books about the topic but he did learn from the internet. I let him proceed at his own pace. He might not be book smart, but he is life smart and Roy always seems to know what to say to support me.

I also want to tell you about Abe. He's another golf buddy and good friend. He is book smart. Abe plays the piano and enjoys chess. He cannot sit still for more than five minutes and my mom would have said he has "ants in his pants."

I wanted to tell Abe about my gender issues too. However, I did not meet with him privately and gradually introduce the topic. We did not have long talks. I skipped all the steps that had proven so helpful for Roy because I was in a hurry and wanted to rush the process. I took Abe for granted.

So one evening I showed up at a party at Roy's house and I was dressed as Bobbi. Abe arrived and walked into the crowded, noisy living room. He did not recognize me. And even though Roy kept telling him over and over who I was, he looked bewildered and I felt badly for him.

Abe appeared overwhelmed and left for home. Later, his wife called to tell me he was troubled and did not know what was going on; he was worried about me. I attempted an explanation over the phone.

Abe and I met privately a few days later and it took a while to repair the damage. We remain great friends and he has been incredibly supportive. I lucked out here because he had every right to have dumped me given the way I initially surprised him.

I was not so lucky with my friend Sarah. Here is an example of how badly a transgender transition can go. Now I know you will remember that she was the very first girl I ever dated; I told you how she broke up with me and married a really nice fellow who owned a Camaro. They ultimately moved to Florida and had a couple of children.

Well Sarah and I remained friends. We contacted each other perhaps every two or three years. She and I would exchange letters and we even met a couple of times for lunch. This occasional connection went on for over forty years. I don't think either one of us ever harbored any thoughts of a romantic future together. We simply enjoyed a very long friendship that was based on mutual concern for each other. We wrote about our ups and downs; I knew about the challenges she had experienced with her husband and her children and she knew about the death of my father, my divorce and my financial struggles. However, I never once told her about Bobbi.

Sarah was the only female friend of my entire life. Oh, I had lots of guy friends but she was the only girl friend I ever had other than my worm-eating, childhood buddy Crystal.

Now please read carefully because this is a classic example of how to ruin a friendship: As my gender confirmation surgery approached, I felt it was about time to tell Sarah all about my situation. She lived out of state and when she answered the phone, Sarah told me she was busy at the moment and could not talk very long.

I should have arranged for another time to talk but I just plowed forward and told her all about my lifelong belief I was a woman. I talked and talked and did not listen. She seemed upset by the news.

I became angry that she was not embracing the new me even though I had only given her all of five minutes to do so. Feeling hurt by her reaction, I fired off an ugly letter and to date, we have not talked for over six years. I have attempted to reach out but to no avail.

There is a take-home message here, especially for transgender individuals. Friendships are some of life's most precious gifts. Each one is unique and can't be taken for granted. If you care about your friend and you finally have to tell them about the real you, take your time. Really think and plan your approach thoroughly as you break the news to your buddy.

Remember, you have known about your story for your entire life. You have a big head start and if you have been hiding really well, they won't have a clue. They are starting from zero. Be sensitive to their needs. Allow them some space. Give them time to process and research and react. Give them a break and forgive them for their pronoun missteps. Lighten up.

I know you are in a hurry to transition but I hope you will heed this warning. If you make it all about yourself in your haste, you will likely lose a friend. I lucked out with Roy and Abe. I completely wrecked a relationship with Sarah because it was all about me and my agenda.

I think I have spent enough time describing some of the land mines related to changing genders. However I have not talked about coming out to my employers. So hold on to your seats because here we go.

Discrimination is always at the door.

*"I will say that, with memoir,
you must be honest."*

ELIE WIESEL

Five

THE CARDBOARD BOX

I have already told you that, at the time of my surgery, I had three jobs.

The first was a very small family practice in Gold Canyon; a concierge-type model where I provided care by making house calls.

The second job involved work as a medical director of two medical-surgical rehabilitation facilities.

My third position was as medical director of a very large hospice company.

In regard to the house call practice, I had to sit down with each and every one of my patients to discuss the entire issue of being transgender. The conversations were tearful, but every single one of these patients renewed with me. They were delighted with my care and were happy I would finally be able to live openly and happily as Bobbi. They all expressed concern for

Lucy and were relieved to learn we were going to stay together as a couple.

Concerning my position at the rehab centers, I was uncertain how the owners would accept my transition. I knew they were members of a very conservative religious community but until the time of my surgery, they had been effusive in their praise of my work performance. Lucy was also assisting me at these facilities as a nurse practitioner and they lauded her work as well. The owners were so ecstatic about my leadership that they purchased health insurance for Lucy and me as an added bonus.

When I began my transition, I started to let my hair grow to ponytail length. I tried to hide my growing breasts. Perhaps several staff members put it all together and spilled the beans because a subtle change occurred in the owner's attitude toward me and they became more formal. We never did have a transgender talk or anything close to it. I was still presenting myself at work as Dr. Bob.

I arrived one day to the rehab facility and everything in my office had been redecorated. I was bewildered and looked at the secretary who shared space with me. I asked her, "I am not sure where my desk is and do you know what the heck is going on here?"

She looked away and burst into tears. She had never behaved like this before. I continued to stand in my old space, obviously dazed.

Within several minutes, I saw the facility administrator walking toward me with a cardboard box. She said she was sorry and told me I had been replaced. Then she handed me the box. It was filled to the brim with a photo of Lucy, my spider plant, my stethoscope, prescription pads, a coffee mug, pens and several books. I said, "Thanks." What was I saying thanks for? I was numb and it was all so confusing.

I felt humiliated as I slithered out of the building. There are no state-wide employment discrimination protections for transgender individuals in Arizona. If there were, I think I would have raised 'holy-hell'.

Even though there had never been an overt conversation about my gender issue, I felt in my heart it had played a major role in my dismissal. I lost a position I really loved and excelled at and Lucy lost her position as well. Our financial crisis had begun.

At least I still had my hospice work. Lucy had applied and found work with them as well. I was still going to work at hospice as Dr. Bob but now I was scared to death I might lose this one remaining job if they found out about me. The thought of being almost completely unemployed at my age was more than I could handle.

So before I left home, I would pull my hair back, take my earrings off, put a breast binder on and wear a baggy shirt. Then I would go see my hospice patients.

I really enjoyed my employment as a hospice doctor. Caring for terminally ill patients and helping their families was the most rewarding activity I had ever done in my entire career. And, as I've pointed out, the income generated was critical.

However, after more than a year of this double life, I could no longer stomach the continued hiding. It was a schizophrenic situation. For example, I would go to work in the morning and care for hospice patients as Dr. Bob. Then I would race home and change into my Dr. Bobbi outfit and see private patients. On many occasions, another costume change was required so I could attend an evening hospice medical director meeting as Dr. Bob. Finally I would return home to end my day as Bobbi.

The moment arrived when I just could not play this game anymore. I was worn out and knew a conversation with my employer was imperative.

I arranged an appointment with the executive medical director who I will call Dr. No, to preserve his anonymity.

This time the discrimination was overt.

I sensed he was a socially conservative individual but couldn't be sure about his attitude toward transgender people. The meeting started out in a very cordial manner. He adored my work and was aware of the rave reviews I'd received from patients and staff alike. After some light banter, I proceeded to tell him all about me, especially my desire to continue providing outstanding care as Dr. Bobbi, not as Dr. Bob.

By the end of the meeting, the thermostat in the room had fallen to forty below zero. I heard every imaginable reason why allowing me to transition on the job would be impossible.

First, Dr. No reminded me I had been hired me as a male and he expected me to honor my contract and remain as a male.

I attempted a rebuttal and pointed out they had accommodated a female medical director who was a Christian when they hired her. Subsequently she had drastically altered her appearance because she had become a Sihk. She was now wearing a turban and a long, flowing gown to the work place. I remarked that she could potentially be a very disruptive element in the organization because of patient or co-worker prejudice. Nevertheless her changes were enthusiastically embraced and my potential changes were rejected.

It appeared that certain changes in appearance and presentation were more acceptable than others; or possibly she was tolerated because she enjoyed civil rights protections that I did not have.

At that point the executive medical director changed direction and offered a new reason as to why I could not work for them as Dr. Bobbi. He was of the opinion I would lose the respect of my teammates if I presented myself as a female.

I strongly disagreed and informed him my private patients had applauded my courage to finally live honestly and they sincerely admired me. I believed my co-workers would react in the same fashion but Dr. No remained skeptical.

Dr. No believed my appearance as a female would be upsetting to the dying patients and their families. He had never seen me dressed as Bobbi but he made some reference about my height, large hands and feet, saying they would be distracting and tip off everyone about my true nature.

Once again I reminded him my private patients in Gold Canyon had found my new appearance to be quite professional and acceptable. They said repeatedly they cared more about my skill and compassion than what I was wearing. I attempted to allay his concerns but to no avail. His mind had been made up. I was crestfallen.

As we wrapped up that first meeting, Dr. No surprised me by saying he would think about my request further and discuss it with other members of the executive team. I was not very optimistic.

In the interim, he forbade me to appear as Bobbi to the staff, whether at work or on my free time. This included an upcoming Christmas party at the home of a team member. He continued to call me Dr. Bob and made no effort to call me by my preferred name of Bobbi, even in the privacy of his office. He was making his point.

A couple of months went by and I continued to change my gender presentation multiple times a day to please the hospice company. Maintaining a life in two genders was exhausting.

Finally the executive medical director contacted me and requested a meeting. He said there had been a new development and he sounded upbeat. As I drove to the meeting, I was filled with hope! For some reason I had a feeling they were going to accept me as Dr. Bobbi and I was anticipating hugging him and everyone else at hospice headquarters. There was a bounce to my step. I had no idea I was about to be dealt a cruel surprise.

Dr. No said the organization had made a decision to terminate my team for financial reasons. They were going to reassign the staff to other teams but, unfortunately, there would be no reassignment for me. He said the winding down of the team would take about two months.

He offered an olive branch and told me there was a chance I might still have a future with the company. He urged me to complete my transition and then perhaps they would think about rehiring me as Dr. Bobbi and use me for vacation relief. It was all very vague. He witnessed my obvious disappointment.

About a month later, Dr. No presented another scenario whereby I could be rehired as Dr. Bobbi. He said they were mulling over the idea of forming an LGBTQ team. There was a possibility I could serve as the medical director of a new group of LGBTQ employees and provide hospice care for terminally ill members of the LGBTQ community. He was not certain this idea would actually be initiated but he wanted my opinion. Dr. No felt this initiative could create a place for me in the organization and it was a perfect solution.

I did not see it the same way. They were telling me indirectly that they did not want me around 'normal' people. However it seemed they were very comfortable having deviant Dr. Bobbi and a team of deviants care for other dying, unwanted deviants in the community.

His suggestion nauseated me. I sarcastically thought to myself, "Maybe they could house the whole bunch of us in a big closet and keep us all out of sight."

It was obvious my employment was coming to an end. So I resigned before they too could hand me a cardboard box. Lucy was left in an awkward situation because she was still employed with them as a nurse practitioner. Within a few months, she resigned as well. It had become clear that tying her career to mine was, as they say, a bad career decision.

I started to look for other work. But at 62 years of age and as a newly-minted transgender woman, it was not going to be easy.

So I did what any other reasonable person would do. I got my clubs out of storage and went golfing. You heard me correctly. I went golfing.

"I am always more interested in what I am about to do than what I have already done."

RACHEL CARSON

Six

Pro Golf or Bust

At Apache Creek Golf Course in 2013

That's right. I went golfing. I did not know how well I could still play but I was going to find out. I had never had this much free time in my life to just hit balls.

It didn't take long to find out I could still play very well. I was breaking par. Now, I wanted to compete again like I had years ago when I won collegiate championships and qualified for national championships. Maybe I could experience another Western States Tour moment one more time.

I applied to the United States Golf Association to compete as a female. I complied with their gender policy and received permission to play. Within a few weeks, I won the Club Championship at Papago Golf Course against some of the best players in Arizona. Three weeks later I won another tournament.

Then I qualified for a national championship in Pennsylvania. The complaints started to roll in. Some competitors suggested I played like a guy and I was too strong. It didn't matter I was the oldest player in the field. Their big concern was the fact I hit the ball longer than any of them and they felt this was not fair.

I thought a lot about their complaints and, in the end, I agreed with them. I had a huge distance advantage and the only thing that somewhat leveled the playing field was my mediocre short game. I did not want to win if other competitors felt it was not fair.

So I stopped playing amateur golf and decided to pursue a childhood dream by becoming a professional golfer. Now I was going to play for money against extremely talented players forty years younger than me.

I needed competition that only tournaments could provide to develop my skills. I found the Cactus Tour, a mini- tour that held events in Arizona, California, Nevada and Texas. It was owned and operated by a fellow named Mike Brown from Tucson. I called him up.

"Hi Mike. My name is Bobbi Lancaster and I would like to compete on your tour." Now in spite of all the female hormones in the world, a transgender woman's voice box does not change anatomically and the vocal quality remains undeniably male.

So I am sure Mr. Brown assumed I was a guy when he replied, "Dude, my tour is for female professional golfers so call somebody else and go play with the men."

Before he could hang up, I blurted out, "Mr. Brown, please don't hang up. I just need a couple minutes of your time. I am a transgender woman and I want to be the best player I can be. I need a place to play and I really need to play on your tour. Please."

There was a prolonged silence. Finally he exclaimed, "Oh, for God's sake...why does this have to happen to me?" He sounded annoyed.

We then had a lively discussion for an hour. He boasted about his Tour and his daughter, who was a professional golfer and a television personality. I told him about my golf dreams.

Eventually I had to bring up the elephant in the room. I told him I'd noticed his web site stated in big bold font that only FEMALES AT BIRTH were eligible to play on his tour. I mentioned how even the USGA, the LPGA and the International Olympic Committee no longer had such a draconian policy like his anymore. Finally at the end of the conversation I asked him, "Well....can I play or not?"

There was a long pause before he replied, "You're in."

I was overjoyed and thanked him profusely. He told me he would never hear the end of it from his conservative friends. We hung up and he changed his web site the very next day.

Of course I was thrilled I had a tour to play on and now I had to get ready. But I kept thinking about the fact I had changed a persons' mind by telling my story, being honest and finding common ground. That initial encounter with Mike planted the thought in my mind that I might end up being an agent of change.

In about a month's time, I would be teeing-it-up at my very first Cactus Tour event. The big day was fast approaching and I wanted to play a practice round to familiarize myself with the golf course. I called the pro shop at the tournament site to obtain a tee time. The assistant pro listened to my request and then said he could not give me a time because the tournament was for female professionals only. He assumed I was a guy.

Here we go again. I did not even try to explain and hung up.

This happened to me frequently when I called for a tee time or a hotel reservation. Intake personnel would always call me 'sir' over the phone and would not allow me to register for preferred room and tee time rates because they were reserved for female competitors. I sounded like a guy on the phone in spite of my best efforts to feminize my voice.

Out of necessity I had to devise a strategy. When I made those types of calls, I would introduce myself as the caddy of Bobbi Lancaster. I would explain I was making reservations for my player and then everything would go smoothly.

I finally arrived to play a practice round before my tournament debut only to find out the pro shop had paired me with two tourists. Their names were Tony and Beth and they were visiting from Minnesota. I hit a 270 yard tee shot on the opening par 4. They were visibly intimidated and proceeded to take at least 10 strokes each and still did not complete the hole. I tapped in for my par and started to look for an escape plan.

I looked back to the first fairway and saw a solo player hitting toward the green we'd just vacated. She had a beautiful swing and I knew she must be a fellow competitor playing a practice round too. On the second tee I informed the couple I wanted to drop back and play with a friend who was behind us. I was telling a little lie but sometimes you have to grasp at anything to save the day. They appeared visibly relieved knowing they would not have to be stressed by my presence any longer. We said our goodbyes and they continued on with their game.

I turned my attention to the young lady who was now walking up to the second tee. She was tanned, athletic and had long brown hair. Did I mention she was absolutely gorgeous too?

I introduced my sixty-two-year-old self and said, "Hello, my name is Bobbi. Are you playing in the Cactus event starting tomorrow?" She flashed the most dazzling smile imaginable and replied, "Yes." Her teeth were so white.

Now I was the one feeling intimidated. I told her I was competing too and asked if I could join her. She responded, "No problem and my name is Nina, Nina Rodriguez." Then she crushed a tee shot up the middle of the fairway and walked confidently off the tee.

I knew right away playing against the young pros was not going to be easy. I had no idea she was a multiple time champion and had been featured on many episodes of the Golf Channel. We made small talk between shots on the second hole. She was very open and easy to be around. By the completion of the third hole I had told her my transgender story and my golf dreams. By the end of the fourth hole she had told me about her family, her girlfriend, the fact she was lesbian and all about her golfing goals. A short time later we just stopped playing and we talked.

Many years have transpired since that first chance meeting. Nina has become one of my best friends. We have played in many tournaments together. I inevitably beat her in the practice rounds but she always scores better in the actual event. She is a winner.

Back to that first professional event, it was a cold Monday morning in January of 2013. Mike introduced me to some of the competitors before play began.

Me and Mike Brown, 2013

When it was my turn to tee off, he proclaimed on the first hole, "Now playing, Bobbi Lancaster from Gold Canyon Arizona." This announcement gave me goose bumps. Everyone clapped and I hit a very good opening drive and played well for the entire round. I had completed the first day of the three day tournament.

Later that evening I received a worried call from Mike. He said, "Bobbi...you have a problem. The media wants to interview you." Apparently a spectator had noticed me competing in the event and felt my transgender presence was not welcome. The fan had then sent an email to the Arizona Republic newspaper requesting they investigate. The senior sports columnist, Paola Boivin, had received the complaint and wanted an interview.

I didn't know what to do. I did not need this media complication while I was working on becoming the best player I could be.

I phoned my family in Canada. They urged me to decline the interview because they knew I had never dealt with the media and I could be overly honest and naïve. They guessed the likely outcome would be an embarrassing, sensational article that would crush me. They were being protective. Of course I talked to Lucy as well. She told me to follow my instincts.

I completed the final two rounds of the competition but I was distracted the entire time because I had a big media decision to make.

Looking good, 2013

At the completion of play, I trusted my gut and called the reporter. Something inside me said it was the correct path to follow.

The next day, there was a film crew and an interviewer at my local golf course watching me hit balls. It was nerve racking and very surreal.

Then Paola arrived at our front door and she proved to be the nicest person in the world. She sat down with Lucy and me in our living room and interviewed us.

Cameras rolled and photographs were taken. That evening I was featured on channel 12 sports, the local NBC affiliate in Phoenix. The breaking news was that a transgender woman was trying to be the first to play on the LPGA Tour! In the blink of a few days, Lucy and I were front page news in the Sunday paper too.

The article was well done and very sensitively presented. It explored the topic of being transgender, the fairness of my competing against cisgender women and the very human story of how our marriage had survived this unbelievable challenge. It was a three page exploration of a taboo topic.

The article appeared all over the country. It was also picked up by USA Today and positive feedback emerged from everywhere. Paola was nominated for a sports Emmy. Here is a paraphrased letter I received from a reader who lives out of state;

Dear Doctor Lancaster

I read the story about you and your wife in the Sunday paper. You seem very smart and caring. About 4 years ago my teenage son approached me to say he felt like a girl. I told him this kind of talk would not be tolerated in this house. He persisted and I kicked him out. I promised I would never talk to him again. I have kept my promise. Then I read about you and now I have a new understanding about transgender people. I realize I've been wrong.

After a few phone calls, I located my son...now my daughter. We had a reunion and we cried. Everything is going to be okay because of you.

Dr. Lancaster, thanks for telling your story and keep speaking out.

Sincerely, Mrs.T.

How many of you have ever received a letter like this? It was the most special thing imaginable. I was helping people and families just by telling my story. From that moment on, I accepted every interview request that came my way. I was now on a mission to help lots of individuals and families.

I can't remember every interview, but they have included Good Morning America, The Huffington Post, talk radio shows, The League of Fans, Freedom for All Americans, NBC Sports, The Golf Channel, Cronkite News, Channel 12, TMZ Sports, the Canadian Medical Post, Sports Illustrated, just to name a few. Many of my friends, including Mike Brown, agreed to be part of these interviews and I am grateful for their outstanding contributions.

One of the interviews was conducted by Jimmy Roberts who has won multiple Sports Emmys with NBC.

Interview with Jimmy Roberts, 2014

He is respected around the world for his journalism excellence. So when his producer called to ask if Jimmy and the Golf Channel could do a story about me, I agreed.

Mr. Roberts flew in from NYC and he and the film crew produced the most amazing documentary about my life and golf dreams. The half hour segment aired multiple times on NBC and the Golf Channel through-out the summer of 2014.

Several things stand out concerning the making of that documentary.

Mr. Roberts and his staff promised they were going to present my story in a sensitive manner. They were not going to look for a sensational angle and they were true to their word. I have the utmost respect for Jimmy Roberts, Paola Boivin and countless other interviewers because, in my opinion, they all have been incredible examples of professionalism and integrity. Not one of them has ever taken a cheap shot or written an inaccurate or salacious story about me.

The performance of a friend who participated in the Golf Channel documentary stands out. Randy is a golf buddy and a patient of mine. On the surface, he is the most unlikely of amigos. He is a self-described Republican-voting, gun-toting, bible-thumping, white, fifty-year-old male. He states his political leanings are "just right of Attila the Hun." He has no particular warm and fuzzy feelings about the LGBTQ community, but he wanted to be interviewed by Jimmy Roberts.

I took a chance and agreed he could be included in the interviews but I was worried about what he might say.

In the end he explained that meeting me had really opened his eyes. I had forced him to think a lot and examine his firmly held beliefs. He talked about being changed by our friendship and how, as a result, he no longer judges people because of an LGBTQ label that might accompany them. Rather, he judges individuals solely on their character and accomplishments. As he said during the documentary, "Bob is now Bobbi and dresses like a woman because she is transgender. So what! She could dress like a duck if she wants to. What matters is that Bobbi is a terrific physician who once made a house call on Christmas evening to assess my sick grand-daughter and treat her ear infection. She is a wonderful and caring person... period."

Randy was not the only one who was changed as a result of our friendship. I know I was changed as well. We might have started from a different place socially and politically. However after many conversations, golf games and laughter, we've found common ground.

Everyone needs a friend like Randy.

Aside from all the interviews, I've also been asked to speak at universities and community colleges, town halls and have participated on a White House Summit panel concerning LGBTQ rights. There have been guest speaker appearances at a lawyer's convention, an international medical symposium and soon I will give the keynote address at McMaster Medical School, my alma mater, during convocation.

One of my most prized possessions is a shoebox full of hundreds of pieces of correspondence I have received. Many are similar to the letter I summarized earlier and all of them thank me for being brave and telling my story. Each writer declares I have really helped them, their family and friends and all encourage me to keep speaking out.

Obviously something I was doing was helping a great number of people and it did not even require a stethoscope or a prescription pad. It was all very humbling and rewarding.

In the middle of this fanfare, I did finish in the top five in several Cactus Tour tournaments and won a few thousand dollars. Because of this modest success, I attempted to qualify for the LPGA Tour. It was an insane thing to do at my age, especially given the fact that media demands meant I had no time to practice. To top it all off, I was injured. I had developed a rotator cuff tear of my right shoulder and tendonitis of my left elbow. In spite of it all I had to try.

I did not receive the okay to play in the four-round LPGA qualifying tournament until two days before it was scheduled to start. I was sitting at home in Arizona, nervously waiting for last minute approval. It had taken a long time to process my application because of the need to comply with their transgender athlete protocol.

On the Sunday morning before the Tuesday start of the competition, the LPGA lawyer, Josh Kane, finally emailed me with the news of acceptance.

Elated, I packed quickly, kissed Lucy goodbye and drove hurriedly from Gold Canyon to Palm Springs,

California. I checked in to my Mission Hills hotel room and slept poorly due to all the excitement.

The next morning while practicing, Heather Daly-Donofrio, the LPGA Vice President of Tour Operations, walked up to me on the putting green. She introduced herself, said she was thrilled I was competing and offered to help me in any way. She is one of the kindest, most professional people I have ever met.

After warming up, I walked to the first tee to start my 11:00 AM practice round. It would be my first look at the course. I paused to admire the sculpture of Dinah Shore near the eighteenth green. She was a long-time, world-class entertainer and supporter of the LPGA Tour who had hosted a major tournament at this very site for many years. Even though she passed away in 1994, she is still remembered and revered.

I attempted to introduce myself to the three Korean professionals also assigned to my practice round time. They did not speak English and I spoke even less Korean. Their caddies intervened and a great deal of excited conversation ensued.

Then one of their caddies approached me and said, in broken English, "They do not want to play with you because you are too old and do not belong." I was taken aback. The language barrier alone made any meaningful discussion impossible and I should have stood my ground and just teed off at my assigned time.

But I demurred and let them play away. I waited for the next group and a possible opening.

The next group could not accommodate me because they already had their quota of four players. It was the same story with the following group as well. There were no openings for me.

I became frustrated and angrily drove my golf cart to the third hole to get ahead of my original Korean group. I played alone and hit multiple shots from various locations. I did not have a caddy and tried to learn the course as best I could all alone.

The evening before the qualifying event started, I attended the player meeting. I was at least thirty or forty years older than all of the competitors. The energy in the room was electric because the future of each and every competitor was riding on their performance that week.

However my future was secure. I was unconditionally loved by Lucy, my family and friends and I was still the doctor to my patients no matter how I played.

In the end my performance did not measure up. I gave it my best effort but my elbow and shoulder ached constantly and I felt emotionally exhausted by all the events leading up to the tournament.

Every round unfolded just like the previous one. I was near par until the final four or five holes and then I stumbled and spoiled everything. I did not qualify for the LPGA Tour but I did gain status on the Symetra Tour. And I made a lot of LPGA friends along the way.

After my final round, I was eating lunch by myself in the clubhouse when I noticed a group of ladies just to my left. They approached my table and one of them stepped forward rather tentatively and asked permission to speak. She told me they were all members at Mission Hills and they had something to say. They had noticed me on the very first day of qualifying because I was so much older than the rest of the competitors. Having done a Google search and review of all the articles written about my life journey, they were in awe of my courage. They were inspired because I was still chasing my dreams at the same age they had given up on theirs.

Because of my example, several of them felt energized and wanted to set some new personal goals. I was very touched. We all enjoyed an emotional hug and a group photo. The impact my story was having on people never ceased to amaze me.

Many people were calling me brave and courageous; others were calling me inspirational. However I was not as tough as you might think. I was crumbling under the pressure of the media attention and having severe difficulties in the glare of the cameras. I was so fearful of posting a mediocre score for the world to see. I had developed 'stage fright'.

A lot of the time I felt I was being reduced to a number: "What did you shoot? How many greens did you hit? How many putts did you take today? What was your score on the front nine?" It seemed like that's all people cared about.

I would hyperventilate to the point of disorientation before tee times. I would cry. Sometimes I would withdraw from a competition at the last minute before it even started.

By now my really good friend, Mike Brown, was aware of my struggles. He urged me to see a sports psychologist. The first one I saw was Chris Dorris in Phoenix. I sat down with him at my first session and we exchanged small talk. He asked how he could help.

I told him my tournament results were well below my usual level of play because of anxiety and self-doubt. I said there must be something 'wrong' with me.

With that, he jumped up from his chair and got right in my face. He told me in no uncertain terms there wasn't anything wrong with me and he never wanted to hear me talk about myself in that way ever again. There was a lot of profanity involved. He believed in me more than I believed in myself.

I will never forget that scene in his office. I saw him multiple times over many months and he helped me with positive thinking, commitment, improved self-talk, mindfulness and a pre-shot routine. He also introduced me to meditation and the concept of enlightenment.

The second psychologist was Dr. Mark Strickland. He took note of the many traumas I had experienced in my early years related to public embarrassment and family violence. He diagnosed me with PTSD and treated me very successfully using a technique called EMDR.

These two individuals provided me with insights and coping strategies I had never known before. They are very much responsible for all the success I now enjoy.

Before I leave this chapter on my professional golf escapades, I have to tell you a story that involved an incident on the Cactus Tour.

I was playing in a tournament at the Wigwam Golf Course, west of Phoenix. I was not performing particularly well and hit a shot into a water hazard and lost the ball. I reached into my bag for another ball and discovered I had forgotten to pack extra golf balls. I checked every compartment of my bag. There were tees, ball markers, extra pencils, divot-repair tools, several gloves, shoelaces, Advil and you-name-it. But there were no golf balls. I could not borrow a ball from a competitor because they were not playing the same brand. So I had to quit the tournament and walked in to tell Mike what had happened.

He thought it was hilarious. He told everyone that, "Bobbi had been disqualified." When they asked him why, he would deadpan, "No balls!" Then he would crack-up laughing.

Even I found his comment really funny. He meant no harm. Apparently he has related this story over and over for the past couple of years. I have to love him for it and we remain good friends.

Well, so much for golf. I had fulfilled my dream of being a professional golfer, but I was not a very good one. I had left it too late in life, but at least I tried.

"I don't want to believe. I want to know."

CARL SAGAN

Seven

SCIENCE FRIDAY

During one of my many trips back to Hamilton, my brother Ken had arranged a family therapy session with a psychologist. That meeting had proven to be invaluable. Everyone was given the time they individually needed to wrap their head around my new reality.

Now it was the summer of 2015 and five years since my big transgender announcement to the family. I was back for another vacation to see them all and play a little golf.

On the second day of my trip, we had dinner at my sister's house. It had been a very relaxing evening and we were clearing the table and enjoying another splash of Chardonnay when my brother Ken turned to me and said, "You know Bobbi, it feels so normal around you now.....just like the old times and I love you more than ever."

I interrupted him to ask, "I sense there is a 'but' coming here. What's the matter?"

He put his hand on my shoulder and said, "I've been doing some reading and I've talked with a lot of people about this transgender thing. They've told me that, in their opinion, it is a bizarre gender choice that some people make. Some say that transgender people are looking for attention. They are exhibitionists. Others declare it is a sexual perversion. Still others say it is an immorality or a psychiatric disorder. Can you help me out here? I want a better understanding."

Before I could answer, my mother chimed in and said, "I've been talking to the priest at my church about you Bobbi. He said you are always welcome to attend mass but you have to talk to him before receiving communion or anything like that. Why do you think he wants to talk with you?"

I looked at my loving but very naïve mother. I knew exactly why he wanted to talk with me. I am sure the pastor wanted to explain why I was disqualified from receiving the sacraments.

For the record, I'll list my most obvious transgressions. My first marriage was a Catholic wedding and I obtained a civil divorce without applying for an annulment. Then I remarried outside the church and changed genders and now I am in a same-sex relationship. I haven't attended mass or holy days of obligation in years and I never did return the library book that was overdue fifty five years ago. I am certain I've been excommunicated several times over and I know where I stand. I am welcome but not included anymore and really have no defense because I broke all the rules.

I was just about to answer my mom's question when Sandy rescued me by saying, "Bobbi...when I worked in your family practice office years ago, I saw how you explained things to the medical students under your supervision. You were amazing and simplified the most complex subject. How would you have taught them about this gender identity issue?"

Ron agreed. "Great question, Sandy. What approach would you have used in presenting this topic, Bobbi?"

I hadn't expected this beautiful Friday evening to take such an unexpected turn, but I couldn't allow the moment to pass. So I had them sit down and then I slipped into my old professor role. I considered my approach keeping in mind none of them were biologists by any stretch of the imagination. Their concept of gender was very basic: people are either born a girl or a boy and no further questions are necessary. It is so obvious.

Were they ever in for a surprise.

I was in a playful mood and announced this very private lesson would be called 'Science Friday with Dr. Bobbi'. They chuckled and then I began.

Turning to my mom I asked, "When you worked in my office as the receptionist years ago, do you remember those two sisters I delivered? The older one was called Jennifer. The younger was Laura."

"Yes, I do remember them," my mother replied. "You really liked that family. The girls were always a hit in the waiting room."

I continued. "Well, I remember Laura's delivery very well because she came out so quickly and of course I said, 'It's a girl,' just like I'd said at so many births before. Those three little words confirmed her biological gender for the rest of her life. She was a female because I had examined her genitals and I had declared it so. It took me less than the blink of an eye to make my assessment. I signed her birth certificate to make it official.

I cared for her for many years. There were well-baby checks and immunizations. I treated her for ear infections and poison ivy. I performed her summer camp and sports physicals and remember how smart, athletic and pretty she was.

"One day when she was about fifteen years old, her mother brought her in to my office because she had a concern. She did not beat around the bush. 'Dr. Bob, Laura has not had her first period and I am worried there is something wrong'.

"Laura was on the Canadian Junior Olympic Team. She was an elite athlete. I told her mother there is often delayed puberty in individuals like her daughter, because they have almost no body fat.

"Her mom had anticipated my response and countered that all of Laura's teammates were the same age and were equally fit and they'd had their first period. In order to reassure this mother, I ordered some basic hormone lab tests on Laura.

"In a couple of days, Laura's results were mailed to my office. Her female hormone level was very low and her male hormone level was extremely elevated.

"This confused me so I called a colleague who specialized in gynecological endocrinology. She instructed me to order a pelvic ultrasound. In several days I received the report and it stated that Laura had no uterus or ovaries. I was stunned.

"The specialist then suggested I order genetic testing and in a week's time I learned that Laura was XY, a genetic male. Now this was extraordinary news.

"A bomb had gone off in Laura's life. Unfortunately she and her family were going to be involved with many specialists and counselors for a long time to come. Her Olympic dreams were shattered."

The living room at my sister's place was so quiet that you could have heard the proverbial pin drop. I broke the silence and said, "I can see by the look on your faces you're confused. You want to know what in the world happened to Laura. How could she be a genetic male when she looked like a female? Well here's the explanation.

"Yes, she was a genetic male and she had testicles. They were located in her abdomen and were making lots of male hormone. However testosterone all by itself is useless unless it can plug in to a receptacle somewhere. It's just like a toaster is useless unless it can be plugged in to an electrical receptacle. These receptacles in a human being are called testosterone receptors.

"There are millions of them and they are located in a number of areas like the brain, the skeletal structure, the voice box, hair follicles, genital area and lots of other places. Their positioning and their ability to bind with testosterone are all under genetic control.

"In Laura's case, none of her receptors were able to bind with testosterone. They were all either missing or not working. The condition is called Complete Androgen Insensitivity Syndrome. Her body, from the time she was in her mother's womb, could not be transformed in to a typical male appearance. Her testosterone was unable to exert its usual effect.

"So her development defaulted to a typical female appearance. This statement is worth repeating. The default gender in a human is female and when a male embryo in the womb is not receiving the anticipated hormonal instructions, it just carries on and develops female structures as best as it can. So on the outside Laura looked like a female and even her brain developed typical female sex center anatomy.

"To be clear, there is a sex center in our brain that deals with gender identity and the male center is anatomically quite different than the female center. This has been confirmed using autopsies and brain imaging studies. I have dubbed this area of the brain our sense-of-self center. I think another appropriate name would be the gender identity center.

"So let me summarize here. This genetic male called Laura, developed a female gender identity brain center and she identified as a girl throughout her entire life. She also looked like a female from head to toe except she had no uterus or ovaries. It was all because the testosterone produced by her testicles was unable to have any effect. Her body was insensitive to it.

"I can tell by your faces that you're absolutely amazed. Like most people, you thought determining gender was so simple. You just look at a baby's genitals and you know they are either a male or a female. However you have to be aware of the fact that occasionally you are going to get it all wrong. In Laura's case, looking at her external genitalia completely missed the complicated biological scene playing out inside her body.

"So where should we have looked to assign her gender? Should we have looked at her genetic profile to answer the question? Or should we have looked at her hormone levels? Maybe we should we have imaged her brain to see if she had a typical female or male gender identity center. Possibly we should have just waited a few years and looked at her skeletal structure and breast development to assign her gender.

"I'm not expecting you to answer these questions and to be honest they are rhetorical anyway. In my opinion, I dislike the entire exercise of assigning gender. However for better or worse in our society everyone has to fit into the gender binary. We could have a lively debate about the need for this construct. Other societies allow for more than two gender designations, but not ours.

"Setting this debate aside, current rules demand that someone has to assign the gender of a newborn. I do feel this duty should be performed by a health care provider. But I also think it should be a temporary designation. There should be an expiration date on this best guess. I am making a serious point here.

"Sometime in the future, as the gender assignment expiration date approaches, the person in question should be asked if they want to confirm their assignment. Just off the top of my head, I think this should be at around 18 years of age. In the end the individual should be the one making the determination. They alone are the expert at this point and they know how they identify."

In Laura's case, if asked, she would have replied, "Of course I am a woman, and my XY chromosomes, high testosterone levels, missing ovaries and uterus be darned."

"That's an incredible story about Laura," said Ken. "I had no idea things like this could happen. But what has it got to do with you?"

"That's a great question, Ken. Actually Laura and I have a lot in common. Listen carefully, because I am about to share one of the biological secrets that explains transgender women like me. All we need is more research but so much is already known.

"First, I am a genetic male, just like Laura. Second, we both had testicles and they made lots of testosterone. However she did not have any working testosterone receptors. That's where we differ.

"It is speculated I DO have working testosterone receptors everywhere in my body, EXCEPT in my brain gender identity center. So I was able to develop typical male features everywhere, but not in my brain. That's why I became six feet tall with lots of muscularity, a beard, a low voice and male genitals. However I couldn't develop a typical male sense of self because my brain defaulted to female gender anatomy just like Laura. The end result is that she and I both identify as women.

"So let's call me a person with Partial Androgen Insensitivity Syndrome. Actually I just coined that term but I think it provides a useful construct and it allows me to explain some very complex biological events.

"I see you nodding your head Ken. Maybe you've grasped this complicated gene, hormone and receptor interplay. How about the rest of you? Are you still with me?"

They all nodded enthusiastically.

"I know you all appear to understand the Laura story. However at the risk of confusing you, I am going to tell you about two other completely different hypotheses that explain the development of a transgender person. So forget Laura for a minute.

"Experts are now aware that the genitals develop in a growing baby during the first trimester of pregnancy. However, the brain gender center develops in the second trimester. Because these events take place at different times, it is possible that they are subject to very different environments in some individuals. For instance their might have been a change in nutrition or a stressful event that occurred. A medicine may have been introduced between trimesters, like diethylstilbestrol. This drug was commonly prescribed during pregnancy from 1940 to 1970 to prevent miscarriages. However it is now known to be an endocrine disruptor. Unfortunately the daughters born of these DES pregnancies have an increased incidence of a rare vaginal cancer and the sons have an increased incidence of being transgender. There are many other so-called endocrine disruptors found in plastics and foods that can disrupt embryo development at critical times. The end result could be a brain gender identity center that does not match the genitals.

"Finally there are experts looking for alternative genetic reasons to explain the transgender phenomenon. They are studying the Y chromosome and they have made some interesting observations. Remember that males have an X and a Y chromosome. The Y chromosome has a gene on it called SRY. This gene or biologic 'computer chip' programs the testicles to grow so they can make testosterone in the correct amounts and at the right time. There is evidence that this gene can be missing, malfunctioning or even be located on the X chromosome in some males. This can lead to problems with testosterone production, delivery and timing in-utero. It is hypothesized this could be a cause of the brain and genital mismatch.

"I know this living room talk gives you lots to think about and there is so much more yet to be discovered. There are likely multiple biological pathways that lead to the development of a transgender individual."

I stopped talking and my family was very quiet. I hoped I hadn't spoiled the evening with my impromptu biology lesson.

My mother broke the silence. I could see tears welling in her eyes. Then she asked the inevitable question. "Bobbi, was it something I did during my pregnancy with you that caused things to go wrong? I am so sorry you ended up being damaged."

I reached for her hand and said, "Mom, you did not do anything wrong. The fact of the matter is you did everything right. You loved and cared for me and you taught me so much. You accepted me more than anyone else in the world. And I thank you for everything you've done.

"However, your question implies there is something wrong with me. I want to make this very clear. Being transgender is not a mistake. There is nothing wrong with me. I am not defective. I am just different. I am a beautiful genetic variation on the theme of being a human being.

"And, aren't we all?"

We finished the dishes, straightened the dining room furniture and talked about tomorrow's plans. Over and over my family thanked me for the Laura story and the rest of my explanations. They get it now… they really get it. They understand how Bobbi came to be.

The evening ended on a really positive note and I can't wait to work on my golf game in the morning.

*"Every moment counts.
Every second matters."*

ELIE WIESEL

Eight

THE RECONCILIATION

The discussion with my family was both emotional and exhausting. I slept like a log and woke to the smell of coffee and the newspaper. My mom was bustling about, preparing for a doctor's appointment and Sandy was going to take her to the clinic. She had waited six months to see an orthopedic specialist and did not want to cancel, though she felt guilty leaving me alone.

"Don't worry about me, Mom. I'll be fine. Once I finish the paper and my coffee, I'm going to drive down to Chedoke to hit some balls. I'll be back by noon and we can have lunch together."

She waved and said, "Okay, and don't forget to read the obituaries. Tell me if you recognize anybody I should know about. See you later. I love you Bobbi."

"I love you too Mom."

I settled in to the high-backed chair, took a sip of my coffee and started to read the obituaries. I remember feeling so incredibly tired and considered cancelling my golf plans. The Science Friday talk had taken a lot out me. I could feel myself fighting sleep as I turned the page.

In the blink of an eye, I was driving her old Toyota down to the golf course. It was a very plain and reliable car. The channel on the AM/FM cassette-radio was set to an oldies station and as I navigated down the highway, Perry Como was singing. I felt like I had entered a time warp.

The route to Chedoke Civic Golf Course was so familiar even though it was fifty years since I had played there as a young teenager. I had worked in the pro shop too. I arrived to find the course all grown up now with mature trees and very green fairways. It looked so small and almost claustrophobic compared with the big modern facilities I'm accustomed to playing these days. There were still two golf courses on the site, the Martin and the Beddoe. My favorite was the longer and more challenging Beddoe.

The parking lot was full. I changed into my golf shoes and with my bag on my shoulder, walked down the hill to the pro shop to get a bucket of practice balls.

I noticed my reflection in the shop window as I strode by. I remember when I was younger how handsome I looked in that window wearing my new golf slacks and shirt. I always looked the part of a young golf pro.

Now it was a surprise to see myself in the window wearing a skirt and sleeveless ladies' golf shirt. Even after 3 years of playing golf as a woman, I was still getting used to being Bobbi and my technique was a little different too. I now had to make a more upright backswing to work around my breast implants. None of my old golf buddies would notice this subtle swing change, let alone understand it.

I walked into the pro shop and literally nothing had changed except I did not recognize a soul. I was disappointed to find out the range was closed so I decided to change plans and play nine holes instead. They told me the tee times were all booked, but if I hurried I could join a threesome on the first tee of the Beddoe course.

I ran to join the group. They had already hit their drives and appeared annoyed that I was joining them. We exchanged hurried introductions and then I teed up my new Titleist golf ball. After a brief stretch and a couple of practice swings, I settled over the ball and hammered it down the middle of the fairway. They all dropped their jaws simultaneously.

I gathered up my clubs and started down memory lane. My thoughts turned quickly to the hundreds of rounds I had played here with friends. I had competed in many tournaments and money games and was the club champion multiple times. I learned how to win at this place and also how to lose graciously too. This was where I grew up.

The others hit their second shots in all directions. My second shot with a wedge to the par four landed and spun left to three feet. I tapped in for a birdie. What a nice start.

On the dog-leg second hole, I had the honor and launched another perfect drive that drew around the corner. I walked off the tee and there was a confident spring in my step. This was going to be a good day.

One of the fellows walked beside me and we made small talk. Then he said, "I really like your swing. It is so similar to my son Bob's."

"How old is your son?"

"Oh, he's 34."

"Is he a member here?"

"Well, he used to be, but now he is a member at Hamilton Golf and Country Club. You know he was a champion here a few times and now he is a champion at Hamilton."

"It sounds like you are pretty proud of him. I am sorry but I didn't catch your name on the first tee."

"My name is Doug. Doug Lancaster."

I stopped in my tracks. It was like a bomb had gone off. I looked at him closely for the first time. I asked, "Sir, could you take your sun glasses and hat off for just a second? Please?" He obliged very cautiously. I looked at him carefully and started to shake. I felt faint. The tears started to roll down my cheeks.

"Are you all right?" he asked, backing up warily.

After a pause, I managed to choke out the words, "No, I am not all right!" I swallowed hard. "You are my father and I am your son, Bob! I am not joking. I know I am older than you but I really am your son. Oh my goodness, this is unbelievable!"

I felt like I was coming unhinged and I must have looked crazy. The other two players rushed over to assess the commotion. I was crying and told them I could not play anymore. I asked Doug to walk me back to the clubhouse. He turned to them and apologized, saying we were having a family emergency. He instructed them to play on.

We started the long uphill walk back to the clubhouse. Doug was quiet and almost peaceful as we trudged along. I was a total mess.

As we walked, I felt the need to convince him I was his son and started to talk. "Doug, I am the oldest of your four children. Then there is Ron, Sandy and Ken. Your wife is Rosalie. Your father was Lorne and your mom was Millicent and they have both passed away.

You were born in Detroit and you served in the Second World War."

Before I could blurt out any more details, he told me to stop talking, breathe slowly and calm down. Then, he announced in a very clear voice, "I know you are my son Bob, even though you look like a woman. Your swing gave you away. A golf swing is as unique as a fingerprint and your swing belongs to Bob and it is beautiful."

Finally we arrived at the clubhouse and sat down in the grill room. He appeared to be somewhat winded. It was relatively empty because everyone was still out on the course.

We gazed at each other for the longest time. Dad looked like he did the day he died back in 1984. He was a little shorter and more grey than I recalled and his hair was thin and a little oily from the Brylcreem he used. His cheeks were somewhat red and scaling because he had not been using the hydrocortisone cream I'd prescribed for his seborrhea. The forehead scar from a drunken car crash years ago was quite visible. My father's hands were hairy and strong. He was wearing his light blue Sansabelt golf slacks with the tobacco burn hole near the right pocket. He had on his usual striped shirt and favorite Arnold Palmer cardigan to complete the look.

He was studying me equally carefully. Then he broke the silence. "What the heck happened to you? And you are so skinny."

I reached out for his hand and held it tightly. It was extremely cold. I kept holding on because I was worried he would disappear.

"I'll tell you about me in a minute, Dad. First, I just have to say that meeting you here does not make any sense. It is the craziest thing that has ever happened to me in my whole crazy life! Where have you been? How did you get to the club? Where do you live?"

He looked at me like I had rocks in my head. He said, "Well, I live on Bowman Street with your mom. You know that. And yesterday, you and I finished building the children's swing set in the backyard of your Scenic Drive home. It was so hot and we went for a swim and then I drove back to my home. I had heartburn so I went to bed early. Now I'm here trying to enjoy a day of golf and we both know how that is going."

I paused. I could not believe what I was hearing. He obviously did not know he had died the night of his heartburn. What in the world was I going to say to him?

I cleared my throat and asked, "Dad, what year is it?"

He answered quickly. "It is August 17th, 1984." I picked up a nearby newspaper and asked him to look at the date on top of the page. He read, "June 20th, 2015." He looked confused and said, "Bob, please tell me what the heck is going on here and don't mess with me."

Well, I was not sure what the heck was going on either. I finally looked him square in the face and said, "Dad, you are not going to believe this but you died on August 16th, 1984. That's almost 31 years ago."

His eyes widened and he looked shocked. He finally managed to say, "Tell me more."

"Well, you were having heartburn and you went to bed. You were actually having a heart attack and experienced a cardiac arrest in your sleep. Mom and Ken found you lifeless in bed. They called me and I raced down to your house at two in the morning. There was nothing I could do. You were very cold and very dead. Your eyes were open and staring so I closed them for you. I called the police and the coroner was involved and an autopsy was done. Your funeral was at Swackhammer's and we buried you at Holy Sepulchre Cemetery in Waterdown. I was too emotional to read the eulogy I had written. I made a temporary marker for your grave until the permanent monument was delivered a few weeks later. Mom is still alive. She is 85 years old and lives in Dundas and she never remarried. Nothing was the same after you left. I am now 65 years old."

He sat there. He displayed no emotion. He wore that darned poker face of his that hid so much when he was younger. Finally after five minutes of total silence, he said, "Okay Bob, I believe you. But you know what this means, don't you?" I shook my head no.

"It means there is no afterlife. You told me I died almost 31 years ago. Well, I should have been in heaven or hell for a long time by now. But I am not in either one of those places. I am here at a golf course with you. Now I think the whole heaven and hell thing was a scam. What a rip-off! I should have known better." He half-laughed and I laughed nervously too.

At this point I had to ask him a question that had perplexed me all these years. "Dad, you knew your father and your uncle had died suddenly of heart attacks in their early fifties. And you had terrible heartburn the night of your death, and yet you did not call me. You didn't go to the hospital, even though Mom urged you to go. You must have known you might have been experiencing a heart problem.

"And after you passed away I found a note in your desk itemizing how you wanted your personal things divided up when you died. It was like you were expecting to die soon. Did you want to die?"

He paused and then said, "Yes, I wanted to die. I had been experiencing heartburn on and off for a while. I knew it was my heart. I did not want to get help. I hoped I would die and I was making plans, like the list you found."

"Why?" I asked him.

"I felt empty and I was sick of trying. I'd had enough. I was not loved by anyone anymore. Even you loathed me. And it was my own darned fault. I had mistreated so many people and I'd hurt too many family members. I only had myself to blame. I was tired of trying to be better while nobody cared or noticed. I sensed there was no forgiveness. So I prayed every day that I would die."

I did not know what to say. His story was unbelievably sad. Finally I opened my mouth and said, "I am so sorry, Dad. I am so very, very sorry."

In an attempt to break the tension I said, "Dad, before we talk any further, how about going to the counter and ordering us something to eat. I am going to call Ken on my cell phone. After we eat, I want you to come with me and see the family. Is that okay?"

"Yes, that's okay by me and when I come back, I want to know what a cell phone is."

I dialed Ken and he picked up right away. I excitedly said, "Ken, it's me. I am down at Chedoke and you won't believe this. Dad is here with me!"

"What did you just say?"

"You heard me correctly. Dad is here with me in the restaurant at Chedoke."

"Bobbi… if this is your idea of a joke, it's really a sick one. Have you been drinking?"

"This is no joke. I am dead serious, so cut out the crap and listen. I know it sounds impossible but he is here. I think it is some sort of paranormal event. I want the family to see him too. Call everybody and get them to your place right now. Tell them to drop everything and I'll see you within the hour."

I hung up. Ken was likely thinking I had lost my mind. Won't he be surprised to see Dad with his own eyes soon?

Dad returned with our lunch. He balanced two hotdogs, two beers and a bag of chips on the tray. He opened the chips in his unique style by tearing the side of the bag open and creating a 'boat.' We laughed as we put mustard on our hotdogs because we both remembered the mustard mess Ron would make every time he got near a hotdog. I asked him why he had ordered a beer for himself after all those years of sobriety. He smiled. "Now that I am dead, what difference does it make? And I've always wanted to have a beer with you." We laughed again.

As we started to eat, Dad said, "Now it's my turn to ask some questions. How are you Bob and why do you look like a woman now?"

I did not know what to say or where to start. I began with, "Dad, after you died, I was numb. I could not cry. I was even angry at you. I kept thinking about all the awful things you had done to Mom and Ron and who knows what with Sandy and Ken. I didn't feel like golfing for a long time and got my teeth fixed with the money you left me in the will. Mary Jo and I moved to Phoenix to try to start over again. We had difficulties with our kids and we went bankrupt. We got divorced and I married

Lucy. I became a U.S. citizen and later had a nervous breakdown and a stroke."

At that point he placed his hand on my shoulder and interrupted me saying, "Stop! Please stop! It's too much information. I can't follow you. You are going too fast and I'm feeling overwhelmed. Just answer me one question. You are a woman now. What in the world happened to you?"

I explained the basics of being transgender and the fact I had always felt like a woman since I was four or five years old. I told him I was confident, happy and peaceful now as Bobbi and that my second wife was my best friend. She had weathered the crisis of my gender change and we would be together forever.

Once again he became very quiet and then he said, "Bob... I mean Bobbi... this is the nuttiest thing I've ever heard of. However I must admit you were always a little different. You were more fragile and sensitive. You enjoyed things like the piano, decorating, gardening and cleaning the house. I wished you had been a little bit more masculine but I did not feel right about forcing the issue."

We took a couple more bites of our hotdogs. Then my dad changed the subject with a question. "Bobbi, you and I had so many adventures here at Chedoke. I want you to think back. What was the one event you remember most that involved you and me?"

I thought about it for a minute. Then I said, "You go first."

"No, I want you to go first."

I thought about it for another minute or two, then I said, "Dad, do you remember when I was fifteen years old, a friend had given me a special ball that apparently Arnold Palmer had played with? I wanted to play a round of golf with it because I felt it would lead to a spectacular score. I rarely lost a golf ball and it seemed like an exciting idea.

"I teed off with you on the first hole of the Beddoe course and hooked my shot into deep rough. We looked for that ball for well over five minutes. It was gone. I was so angry I had lost it on my first swing. I was swearing and complaining and whining.

"You were in the middle of the fairway and preparing to play your second shot. You obviously could hear me feeling sorry for myself. And you snapped. You picked up your ball abruptly and started walking back to the clubhouse. You said something like you were sick and tired of listening to me piss and moan about the lost ball. You told me as far as you were concerned, I could just go screw myself. You just kept walking. You went to the parking lot, dumped your clubs in the trunk and drove away!

"Well, I was in no mood to play either, so I walked back to the clubhouse too. And then I had to keep walking the four miles home. I walked and I walked with my clubs on my shoulder. The spikes on my golf shoes clicked on the sidewalks as I trudged along. People stared at me. Drivers honked their horns because I looked out of place.

"While I was walking glumly along a side street, a very elderly lady called out to me from her front porch. She was waving her arms frantically. I put down my clubs and clacked up her driveway. She could barely speak because she had locked herself out of her house. She did not know what to do.

"I tried all the doors and sure enough, they were locked. Then I noticed she had a milk box near her side entrance. I opened the small door and pushed on the inside door. Thankfully it was unlatched. I moved a garden chair over to the opening and stepped up on the chair and entered the milk door head first. I wriggled through the very tiny confines and fell onto her kitchen floor. Then I walked to her front door and let her in.

"She was ecstatic. She hugged me and wanted to give me some money. I declined the dollar bill. I just hoped that God had been watching and that this, along with a thousand other good deeds I had done, would prevent me from going to hell.

"I finally made it back home. You were in the living room having a beer and watching television. You did not even look up. We continued to act like nothing had happened earlier in the day. We never spoke about the fact that you had left me stranded. It was so weird. I know we had started out with the best of intentions of having a happy father-and-son day, but it certainly did not work out that way.

"Okay, Dad, now it's your turn. What episode do you remember the most?"

He did not hesitate for even a second. He said, "Bobbi, I'm sure you remember winning the Martin Club Championship at Chedoke for the second time. In the final round you had a big lead. I was in the clubhouse drinking with my buddies and bragging about you. Then we all went out to watch you play the final hole.

"You'll remember the 18th hole was a short, risk-reward par 4. All of the contestants before you were going for the green with their tee shots. Some hit their shots out of bounds just to the left of the green. Others were blocking it to the right and down a hill into deep grass and trees. One contestant actually hit the green and two putt for a birdie. He was a hero.

"Then you appeared on the tee 275 yards away. I told everyone around me you would go for the green. And you played safe! You laid up short, pitched on, two-putt and made your par. You won the tournament by something like ten shots but I was so embarrassed because you had played the final hole like a wimp.

"You walked off the green with a big smile and every-one was congratulating you. Then you approached me standing behind the green, looking for a hug. All of my friends were watching. I told you how disappointed I was in you and called you a coward for not trying to drive the last green. I said I was ashamed of you.

"In an instant I realized how much I had hurt you. I was so sorry about what I had said but there was nothing I could do to fix it.

"That's my most memorable and regrettable memory of you and me at Chedoke. I wish I could have a redo of those few minutes."

We were silent again. It was hard to say anything after that exchange. We picked at our lunch. I looked up to discover him staring right at me.

He said, "I should have told you this a long time ago but I was just too selfish and caught up in my own problems. I loved you back then, Bobbi, and I was so proud of you. And I love you even more now. I really do."

"I love you too Dad and I want to apologize for shoving you around and threatening to kill you so many years ago."

We looked at each other and then started crying and hugging. What a spectacle we were making of ourselves in the grill room that was filling rapidly with customers. Then he said, "You look great and I love your teeth. I also like calling you Bobbi. It suits you."

By then, it was time to leave for Ken's house. I paid for lunch and we headed out the door. He stopped, and with a mischievous grin asked if I could hit one more drive for him.

"Sure Dad."

"What's your handicap now?"

"Scratch."

His grin widened further as he marched me down to the first tee.

There were several groups waiting to play. He walked right up to them and said he was not trying to butt in, but he wanted to see his daughter hit just one more shot for him. Everyone stepped aside and I took out a new sleeve of balls and grabbed my driver. I ripped the first one 275 yards down the center of the first fairway with a tight little draw. I hit the same shot with the second and the third ball. Everyone clapped. Then Dad and I walked away to the parking lot. He was beaming like a big Cheshire cat and I could see how proud he was.

First tee of the Beddoe course, 2015

When I asked him where he was parked he couldn't remember. So we loaded our clubs in Mom's car and he sat in the passenger seat. Then I realized I had left my cell phone on the table in the grill room. I told him I'd be right back.

I was gone 30 seconds. When I returned he was not in the car. He was missing. I ran back to the clubhouse to see if he had followed me but he was not there. I checked out the men's locker room. Negative. I was beginning to stress.

I raced outside and saw the two fellows we had originally played with. They had just finished nine holes. "Have you seen Doug?" I asked them. They had not seen him since he left with me on the second hole.

Now I was in a full panic. My mind was racing as I hurried to the pro shop and I was silently begging, "Please, please, please, Dad. Do not leave me again. I don't think I can get over you leaving a second time. Please be in the pro shop, Dad."

Sure enough, the pro said that Doug had been there just a minute ago and he had done a strange thing. He had handed them his clubs and said he wasn't going to need them anymore. He asked if they would give his equipment to a deserving young junior. Then he left.

I asked the pro what direction he had headed but he did not know. I wondered if he'd ever seen Doug before. "Oh yes," he said. "He would show up as a single every month for years and insist on playing the Beddoe course. Each time he would ask if Bob was playing today. We had no idea who he was talking about but he was clearly looking for someone."

I looked around for a little while longer but I knew in my heart that Dad was really gone for good this time.

❖　❖　❖

At that very moment, I awoke with a start, knocking the cup of cold coffee to the floor. The newspaper went flying. I was perspiring and momentarily disoriented.

I realized I had fallen asleep. I had not even left for the golf course yet. The entire encounter with my father had felt so real even though I had obviously been dreaming.

But now that I was awake, I had this bad feeling my father was in trouble and I had to check things out at his gravesite. I put away the paper and cleaned up the spilled coffee. Then I ran to my mother's car and drove far too quickly. It took me fifteen minutes to get to the cemetery and I screeched to a halt, expecting to see the monument upended and an eruption of earth and casket parts everywhere.

Instead, everything was in its place. There were a few people tending to flowers nearby. I looked at my Dad's stone, read the inscription for the thousandth time, and picked a few weeds. There were a couple of squirrels playing nearby. A giant swallowtail darted in and out of view. It was just a sunny and peaceful day.

The dream involving my father did not happen by accident. I clearly needed to talk with him. He never knew about my transgender struggles and I never understood the demons he wrestled with. We had a conflicted relationship and we should have settled our differences a long time ago. We had both put off that courageous conversation until the time was right.

Unfortunately, his sudden and unexpected death robbed us of any chance of fence-mending.

It taught me several valuable life lessons:

First there is the one called doing the right thing and doing it now because there may be no tomorrow. As a result, when my actions at times result in unintended slights, I now apologize quickly and say special things without delay.

There is another that states there is no place for grudges. Life is too short to be preoccupied with petty annoyances.

Still another reminds me of the precarious nature of life. We are all literally a medical moment away from being silenced.

Finally, I've learned living with no regret is a lot easier than living with no chance of reconciliation. I should never have allowed the relationship with my father to end the way it did.

Dad's grave at Holy Sepulchre Cemetery, in Waterdown Ontario

"How many times can a man turn his head
And pretend he just doesn't see?
The answer, my friend, is
blowing in the wind.
The answer is blowing in the wind."

Bob Dylan

Nine

Blowing in The Wind

I am reminded on a daily basis that my personal hourglass is, at best, only twenty percent full. There is a daily bombardment of ads encouraging me to buy Medicare supplemental health insurance. Infomercials directed at people my age repeatedly tout the value of reverse mortgages. AARP frequently sends me membership material, though I have resisted signing up. Store clerks remind me I am eligible for a senior discount. Social Security just sent me a statement clarifying what my monthly benefit would be if I applied now. And of course, I have to start every day with an Aleve, but at least I don't have to worry about low testosterone.

I might feel young but one look in a mirror confirms the reality of my situation.

So it should not have come as a surprise when, at the conclusion of one of my presentations, I was asked a thought-provoking question usually reserved for old people.

The college student approached the microphone and she was obviously nervous but wanted to tell me how inspired she was by my courage and resilience in the face of all the adversity.

Aside from that, she wanted me to list the principles I have adhered to that helped me navigate the challenges life has presented. She was hopeful I would share my secret formula for success with the class.

It reminded me of the question we always ask really old people: "What did you do that allowed you to live for a hundred years?" Usually the response is counter-intuitive and unhelpful like, "I ate a raw egg every day my entire life," or "I enjoyed a shot of whiskey and a cigar every night for the past fifty years."

I almost dismissed the student's question because I would rather answer it in fifteen years when I am older and wiser.

However I paused and decided to give it my best shot. It took me a minute to organize my thoughts and I stalled by thanking her twice for asking such a great question. Finally, here is what I said:

"First, you need to have *empathy*. This attribute separates us from all other life. In my opinion, it is the definitive answer to the question of what it means to be human. Empathy requires you see things from the other perspective. This seems to come naturally for most people. However, if it is a concept you feel awkward about, you can work on it by simply imagining walking in the shoes, or paws, or claws of others, if you follow my drift.

"In the end empathy can help you accept all human beings as equals and place their needs in front of your own. Fair play will govern your negotiations. It can enable you to look at all creatures, great and small, through a different lens. Your life can be more joyful and enriched when you approach even a tree with the respect and dignity it deserves. Make empathy your best friend.

"Second, you need to find *work* that is fulfilling. You have to know you are contributing. It is wonderful to feel you are pulling your own weight.

"Work focuses your life. It allows you to be more in control of your destiny. If you are lost and you don't know what your work should be, then reflect on your childhood. When you were a kid, almost certainly there was something that consumed all your time and effortlessly held your attention. Whatever that was, it is a huge clue and should help clarify a career path.

"Third, you need to ask *why* a lot. You have to be inquisitive. There are no stupid questions and everything should be on the table. Try to understand how things work and think outside the box. Find multiple solutions for the same problem. You can start by asking yourself why you think Dr. Bobbi wrote this book to begin with. What was the motivation?

"Fourth, you need to seek *companionship*. It is imperative that you are connected. It could be with a spouse or a best friend. It could even be with a dog or a cat or some other pet, unless you have asthma or allergies. It is comforting to know you are loved and needed. It is equally powerful to love and care in return.

"Fifth, you need to make *play* an integral part of your life. It is important to smile and laugh and simply goof off. It helps you recharge and it inevitably leads to people and conversations and different points of view. Friendships can blossom.

"Personally speaking, laughing and having fun have been difficult for me as I get older. More than a few friends have encouraged me to smile more. They tell me I look grim and appear to take myself too seriously. I think they make a valid point and I am working on playing more. My face hurts after laughing a lot so I can tell I am out of practice.

"Finally, there is great value in just *showing up* for life. You have probably heard that one of the keys to success is simply sticking around. I agree wholeheartedly with this sentiment. Talent is great but perseverance and hard work are more important. Recommitment to your goals every day is equally important.

"So there you have it. Practice empathy, find meaningful work, ask 'why' a lot, seek companionship, schedule some play, and just show up. The list is not very scholarly but it summarizes the basic principles that have helped me get to where I am today."

Conspicuous by its absence is any mention of religion. By now all of you know I was raised in a Roman Catholic family. You are aware there is a tension between me and the church, to put it politely. I abandoned my interest in Catholicism and for that matter, all traditional religious institutions and their dogmas a long time ago. I guess you could say I am an evidence-based person to my core. However I also consider myself a very spiritual person.

To be fair, I have observed some very touching and compassionate moments initiated by a variety of non-traditional church communities and faith leaders. The power of their message about love and acceptance cannot be overstated. These communities appear to be less concerned with rules and dogma and more concerned with simply loving thy neighbor. Bravo!

I am approaching the end of my book and looking forward to presenting the final chapter. However there is other important business I want to share it with you.

Once I started living my true and authentic life, I witnessed things that really upset me. I couldn't help but notice how many in the transgender community were really struggling and in trouble. I'll give you several examples:

In Arizona, if you are a transgender teenager and you come out to your parents, you have a one in four chance of being kicked out of your home. You heard me correctly; one in four young people are told to get out.

I have met these 'statistics.' They are lost and often end up hungry and homeless. They are bullied and assaulted. They quit school. Some give up and commit suicide while others resort to survival crime. Too many end up being sex trafficked because, at some point, they will do almost anything for a meal, some clothing and shelter.

I have learned something else. Transgender women like me have a one in twelve chance of being murdered. And if I were a transgender woman of color, the chance would be one in eight. Now this is a very sobering and frightening fact. I could present even more depressing statistics.

Aside from this, I have become aware that many state legislatures across the United States appear to be biased against the LGBTQ community. By the end of 2016 there were 204 anti-LGBTQ bills introduced in over thirty state legislatures in that year alone. Since President Trump was elected, legislators appear to be even more emboldened and new bills are rolling in as I write.

These bills revolve around several themes. Religious Freedom laws or some variation on the theme are the most common. Briefly, these proposed statutes would allow for LGBTQ discrimination. If a person feels that an LGBTQ individual's lifestyle is contrary to his/her firmly held religious belief, he/she can deny service to that individual. The logical conclusion is that First Amendment religious rights trump my basic human rights to life, liberty and the pursuit of happiness. It's tantamount to saying transgender people like me are not created equal and should not enjoy legal protections around employment, housing and public accommodation and things that everyone else takes for granted.

Other proposed laws would allow a state to prevent municipalities in their jurisdiction from passing LGBTQ protective ordinances. These are called Pre-emptive bills.

Some proposed laws are so-called Bathroom Bills. They would force people like me to use the restroom corresponding to my gender assigned at birth and not the gender to which I identify. They are designed to keep the public safe from people like me. The proponents erroneously portray transgender women as sexual predators. They suggest all we think about is attacking or taking advantage of women and young girls in bathrooms and locker rooms. Their message of fear seems to sell well.

There is absolutely not a shred of evidence to support this assertion. The only people that are placed at risk by these bathroom laws are transgender individuals.

Of course, there are and always will be predators in society. They are called criminals and there are already laws and police in place to help protect us from them.

Other legislators propose bills that would stop funding for HIV education and prevention and redirect the money to programs that try to 'cure' a gay or transgender person. This is called conversion therapy. Every major medical organization has denounced this so-called therapy as bogus. Not only does it not work, there can be serious side effects. It is impossible to change the in utero wiring of a person's sexual orientation or gender identity any more than you can change their blood type or eye color or handedness.

So these are just some of the things I've observed since coming out. I've already told you how I used my unexpected position as a minor-celebrity athlete to educate and hopefully influence public opinion and acceptance through the media. But was I doing enough?

Even though at times I felt emotionally spent, a retirement involving golf, reading, gardening, hiking, and playing the piano seemed empty. I felt compelled to help the transgender community even more.

At about this same time, I had a further revelation. Transgender individuals were not some single-issue, monolithic group that all looked like me. They had rich and complicated lives and often faced multiple layers of discrimination.

For example, they could be a person of color. They could be members of any faith community or perhaps even atheists. The transgender person could be young or old, poor, unemployed, on welfare, disabled, incarcerated, uninsured, addicted, an immigrant, a refugee, homeless or even sex-trafficked.

Every one of these groups experience their own discrimination and persecution. Many transgender people don't just have gender battles to fight. Rather, they have some or all of the issues I listed above to contend with and it can be overwhelming.

It became obvious I couldn't just champion for transgender acceptance and equality without advocating for many other civil rights issues too. I had a lot to learn.

I was eager to move forward but I lacked a mentor. I needed some guidance. As if by magic, several individuals figuratively entered my life and showed me the way. I want to introduce them to you:

The first is Elie Wiesel. Elie passed away in 2016 at 87 years of age. He was a Romanian-born Jew who survived Nazi concentration camps during the Second World War. His family was not as fortunate.

He was silent about his experience for many years and then he found his voice. He spent the rest of his long life shining a light on discrimination wherever he found it. This Nobel Prize winner spoke about the Holocaust to honor all the victims, lest anyone forget. He railed against hate and oppression in all its ugly forms. He most enjoyed speaking to young people.

He warned there is something just as egregious as discrimination. It is *indifference* and *silence* in the face of witnessed oppression. Here is a sampling of some of Elie's more famous quotes:

"Wherever human beings endure suffering and humiliation, we must take sides. Neutrality helps the oppressor, never the victim. Silence encourages the tormentor, never the tormented."

"Indifference, to me, is the epitome of evil. I swear never to be silent."

"The opposite of love is not hate, its indifference."

"Because of indifference, one dies before one actually dies."

Another individual who has been instrumental in helping me find my voice is Audre Lorde. Audre died in 1992 and was an African-American writer and poet. She was also a feminist, a lesbian and a civil rights activist.

With powerful words, she expressed anger and outrage in the most eloquent way. She was not silent in the face of discrimination. Here are several of her quotes:

"When we speak, we are afraid our words will not be heard or welcomed. But when we are silent, we are still afraid. So it is better to speak."
"Oppression is as American as apple pie."
"We must be the change that we wish to see in the world."
"Your silence will not protect you."
"It is not our difference that divides us. It is our inability to recognize, accept and celebrate those differences.

Finally there is Toni Morrison, the American novelist, editor and Professor Emeritus at Princeton University. Toni was awarded the Nobel Prize in literature. I have learned a lot from her. Here are a few of her quotes to help you get acquainted:

"Make a difference about something other than yourself."

"If you surrender to the wind, you can ride it."
"You wanna fly? Then you got to give up the shit that weighs you down."

These individuals made a huge impact on me and bolstered my resolve.

Another piece to my advocacy puzzle also fell in to place. Remember the old Chinese proverb, "When the advocate is ready, the platform will appear?" In my case, the Human Rights Campaign became my new and unexpected platform. This non-profit is the largest civil rights organization advocating for LGBTQ rights in the United States and the world. They noted my efforts and presented me with their Equality Award in 2015. Soon after, I was elected to their national board of directors where I attended meetings in Washington D. C. and lobbied on Capitol Hill as well as the Arizona State legislature.

Aside from HRC, I continue to speak-out privately against discrimination. However the way in which I choose to use my voice is different. Let me explain:

In my opinion, the current tactics being waged to win the 'war' between the social conservatives/religious fundamentalists and the LGBTQ community are mutually destructive.

The one side portrays LGBTQ individuals as immoral, sinful, delusional, perverted and criminal. They appear to think we represent a fad and are attempting to conscript and corrupt society. They try to pass laws to remind us we are not equal.

The LGBTQ side is equally strident in portraying their adversaries as uncaring, vile, hateful, rigid, ignorant and judgmental. They demand the passage of non-discrimination laws.

The line has clearly been drawn. Each win for one side is a loss for the other. Appeals of appeals are the norm and so it goes, around and around. This appears to be the way disputes are handled in our society.

But there has to be another way. I don't really want someone to serve me, or rent an apartment to me, or cater my wedding because they are legally forced to. Rather, I want them to provide services because they want to.

How can we ever get to that point? For starters, both sides need to talk, and I don't mean in court or by waving placards and shouting slogans at protest rallies. We need to talk and listen and really try to understand where both sides are coming from. We need to be open to facts. Myths and misconceptions have to be dismissed. Space needs to be made for apologies and forgiveness.

When we declare, 'it is self-evident that all men are created equal', we need to take time to reflect on what that really means.

When we drill down and discover the fundamental theme at the core of all religions, we always find the same welcoming message of love and acceptance. We need to internalize this.

I know the solution to the impasse appears to be so simple but it really is that simple. In the end, both sides need to realize we are all incredible, unique, biological variations on the theme of being human. Our diversity should be embraced and celebrated.

Or we can keep drawing that line and continue meeting in court. I would rather talk and listen and find common ground.

Speaking during a Phoenix Valley Leadership Class

Speaking at a Town Hall in Prescott AZ

Bobbi with Lucy during a presentation

Volunteering with HRC

Speaking with Hillary for the first time in 2016

Bobbi and Hillary 2016

Lobbying on Capitol Hill with HRC 2015

Receiving the HRC Equality Award 2015

❖ ❖ ❖

I have provided you with ample information about transgender individuals. You are more familiar now with how they live and why they hide, what a transition is like and the discrimination they experience. You know a great deal about the biology too. Now I have a few questions I'd like you to think about.

How will you react when you hear about a co-worker who is transitioning in your department at work? Will you be supportive? What might you say?

Imagine you have just been informed that a transgender person is applying for a position in your company. Will you judge them on their merits or will you overlook their application just because?

What will you say to your best friend when they tell you their daughter has just informed them she has always felt like a male and wants to transition? Your friend will be looking for support and maybe some guidance. What do you imagine saying now that you have read this book?

If your favorite dentist tearfully tells you he or she is transgender and is hoping you will understand and be accepting during their transition, how will you react? Will you be shocked? Will you simply find a new dentist?

And finally, how will you vote when you are staring at a proposition in a voting booth that would discriminate against the LGBTQ community? Which box will you check? I hope that I have helped you with your decision.

❖ ❖ ❖

O f course LGBTQ issues are important, but there are so many other really important causes.

I wonder what you're interested in and concerned about. Is it baby seal hunts in Canada? Or is it voter rights, healthcare reform, legalizing marijuana, distracted driving, gun safety, pipelines through reservations, global warming, fracking, homelessness, human trafficking, Black Lives Matter, women's rights, helping refugees? The list is endless.

My hunch is you have seen something or read about an issue and it has disturbed you but you have looked the other way. It is probably something you are knowledgeable about and you know you should have spoken out. However something held you back.

My hope is you will start humming Blowing in the Wind. My dream is someone like Audre Lorde, Elie Wiesel or Toni Morrison will start whispering in your ear in an attempt to shake you from your silence or indifference.

If these individuals are not able to get you fired-up, then make plans to visit Washington, D.C. and climb the stairs of the Lincoln Memorial to spend an hour reflecting. Visit the other Memorials too. If you happen to be in Birmingham, allow for some time to follow the Freedom Walk. Seek out opportunities like this because they are all around you.

Feel inspired, be courageous, take a big breath and then speak out. Do something. If not you, then who will help?

❖ ❖ ❖

Finally I have to ask you a question. Do you see yourself in me? Have you bought in to a narrative that there is something wrong with you, like I did for all those years?

If you have, then I am concerned. You must push back. You can't accept someone else's conclusion that you are stupid, deficient or don't matter. All of that kind of talk is wrong and untrue.

Here is what I do know about you:

At one time you were an amazing, magical child just like me. You had unlimited potential. And then you were judged and placed in some category. You lost some confidence and developed self-limiting beliefs.

I am here to encourage you to follow my path and stop hiding. Stop any destructive self-talk you may be engaged in. Please hold your head up high and conduct yourself with confidence. You are unique and you have great worth.

In my case, it took the better part of a long life to finally shake off the chains I had allowed others to place on me. After a painful journey, I am back to where I started and now I feel like that ten year old Robbie again. The sky is the limit once more.

It should be for you too.

"Courageous people do not fear forgiving for the sake of peace."

<small>NELSON MANDELA</small>

Ten

Forgiveness

This book started with a story about my parents. And I am going to finish it with a few comments about my mom and dad and how our relationship has evolved.

Recently I flew back to Hamilton to celebrate my mother's eighty seventh birth day. I dislike flying because it has become increasingly more difficult to fold my slim, six-foot arthritic frame into a cramped airplane seat. And the unfolding, five hours later, is an exercise in physics and origami.

My mom looked great. However she is challenged orthopedically and struggles with word-finding and her short term memory.

Mom is at a stage where she wants to get rid of clutter and give away things. She does not want a mess left behind for her four children when she passes on.

We were going through some old clothes and boxes. She was throwing away items from a kitchen drawer when she discovered a small black object. She handed it to me, asking if I knew what it was.

I had never seen anything like it before. It looked like an inhaler used by asthmatic patients. I tried to read the label on the side of the canister but it was too small to make anything out and I did not have my 'readers' with me. So I did what any curious person would do and pushed the top of the 'inhaler' to see if it still worked. A puff of something discharged in my face. Within a second, I was coughing violently and could not see. Tears were streaming down my face. My nose was running and Mom was in distress as well.

The 'inhaler' contained pepper spray! It had been given to Mom years ago by a friend who was concerned she lived alone. I guess he felt she needed some mace for personal protection.

Mom and I stumbled out of her condo gasping for breath in the hallway. We were gagging and I felt like I would never recover my breath. I improved sufficiently to run back inside and open the windows and a patio door before tumbling back out.

We could not return to the condo for over an hour. I felt so stupid. Later on all we could do is laugh.

Mom and I laugh a lot more together now. We are more like peers who share our secrets.

After this crisis, my trip became almost ordinary. Oh, I did plug her toilet that never did flush worth a darn. She does not own a plunger. Much to her embarrassment, I went next door to borrow one. She was mortified that I had talked to her neighbor about toilets. I gently tried to tell her to get over it.

The morning after the mace event, we went shopping together. We closed and locked the door and proceeded to the elevator. That's where the fun and games began. As we waited for the elevator, a neighbor approached to stand with us. She and my mom exchanged small talk. Then the neighbor turned toward me and asked, "Who's this?"

My mom replied, "She is my daughter from Arizona". She boasted, "She used to be the most popular doctor in Hamilton. She delivered hundreds and hundreds of babies."

Still talking, she added, "He is just visiting for a week. She still sees patients in Gold Canyon, Arizona and they all love her just like they did in Hamilton. He serves on many boards and she's a famous golfer too. Her name is Bob. I mean Bobbi."

By this point, Mom's neighbor was completely confused. Mom was lucky to have not been arrested by the 'pronoun police.' Sometimes I even get confused listening to her and start calling myself Bob again. In the end all that matters is we love each other.

When I returned to Arizona from that trip, I had to catch up on the weeding in my garden. I have planted and grown things for over sixty years and I can usually grow anything, anytime and anywhere. Yes, I have a green thumb. I wish my mom could watch me pick lettuce for a dinner salad tonight and for our tortoise in the morning. Mom admires my farmer instincts and laments she does not have a garden of her own anymore.

However, the one place I cannot grow anything is around the monument marking my father's grave. For over thirty years I have tried to get something to take root there. I have planted annuals and every perennial imaginable but they all wilt and die. I am embarrassed to say that at times I have resorted to artificial flowers.

In some ways, I think my horticultural failings at his gravesite are symbolic of the failure of our relationship. We just never seemed to click. We never flourished together.

Next spring I am going to return with a new landscaping approach. My plan is to plant hardy and cold tolerant shrubs around his marker and forget the flowers. I think this will be the winning solution.

I did have another father in my life. Father Keegan was the priest who had heard my confession so many years ago. He was the one who changed my life and crushed my spirit. Because there was unfinished business between the two of us, I wanted to talk with him, adult to adult and outside of a confessional. I wanted forgiveness.

So I searched for Father Keegan on the web, not knowing whether he was still alive. I had been fourteen when I was his lead altar boy and I guessed he would have been in his late thirties at that time.

After a great deal of detective work, it appeared I had located him. He was still alive and in his eighties, living in an assisted care wing of a convent, just outside Hamilton, Ontario.

The nun who answered my call was thrilled the priest would have an old altar boy as a visitor. Apparently he did not have many visitors anymore and I arranged a meeting time. She told me he was still alert mentally but he had been hobbled by a stroke several years before. I told her that Father would remember my name as Bob Lancaster but he would likely not recognize me because a lot of time had passed. Of course he did not know I was Bobbi now. In fact I was apprehensive I would not recognize him either.

I flew to Canada from my home in Arizona, stayed at my mother's condo and enjoyed a visit with her. Father Keegan resided just thirty miles away and my appointment was on the third day of my trip.

I rehearsed the entire meeting over and over. I memorized my questions and even anticipated his answers. Here is how I thought the encounter would unfold:

"Hello, Father Keegan. My name is Dr. Bobbi Lancaster and I was your lead altar boy back in 1964. I would like to talk to you for a few minutes. Is this a convenient time?"

"Yes, this is as good a time as any. I was expecting Bob Lancaster to visit with me today and you are a woman. I am confused because there weren't any altar girls until the 1980's. So I doubt you served mass with me in the 60's."

"I realize this is confusing, Father, but I used to be Bob and now I am Bobbi. I am a transgender person. Have you ever heard that term before?"

"Yes, of course. I know all about it because I have been watching a television show called *Transparent* with the nuns every week. Are you certain we've met before?"

"Oh yes, we have met and I'll prove it to you. Remember the Easter Mass when you were carrying that six-foot lighted candle into church? I was walking right beside you with the incense. You bent forward as you ducked under a doorway and the hot, melted wax at the top of the candle spilled onto your hands. You stiffened in pain as your fingers turned bright red and I let out a little yell. I don't think I swore but I might have.

"You just carried on with the procession as if nothing had happened. Later you said you did not want anything to detract from the solemnity of the moment. I could not believe your pain tolerance. I helped clean the waxy mess after the ceremony."

"Okay, I believe you now. No one else in the world would know that story. I am convinced you were my server. By the way, you did swear. I distinctly heard you say, 'Oh shit!' under your breath."

We both laughed. The ice was broken.

My rehearsal was going well. I hoped the real meeting would not be a disappointment. Now I wanted to practice the most contentious questions and anticipate his responses:

"Father, do you remember my confession when I told you I felt like a girl?"

"Of course I do. It was one of the most unusual discussions I ever had as a priest. In fact I thought about that conversation over and over for years. I often wondered how things had worked out for you. Over time, I came to the conclusion I had been too harsh and dogmatic. People like you were not sinful. You were just different and brave. You were created in God's image and all you wanted was acceptance and love. You opened my eyes, Bobbi, and I learned to be more empathetic because of you."

Wow! Maybe I should just enjoy his imagined response, leave well enough alone and cancel the meeting.

I hoped Father Keegan would seize the moment and say, "Bobbi, I want to apologize, because I am sorry for what I said to you years ago. Is there anything I can do to repair the damage?"

Those words would be my cue to pull him close and say, "Father, it appears you have struggled, too, because of the way you handled our confessional meeting years ago. I accept your apology and I forgive you, Father. Now let us both go in peace."

I could picture Father nodding in agreement and gently holding my hand for a long time. He would tell me I was forgiven too.

That was my final dry run. All that remained was the actual meeting at 9:00 the next morning.

I arrived right on time. The receptionist at the convent was initially somewhat confused because she had been told a former altar boy was scheduled to meet with Father Keegan. I explained I was Bob years ago and now I am Bobbi, but before I could continue she told me to shush. She said, "We all know about transgender people because we have read about Caitlyn Jenner and watched documentaries on the educational channel."

She guided me through a maze of corridors and smiling, elderly nuns. My heart was pounding just the way it was before my confession years ago. This was going to be a big moment.

Finally we arrived at Father's Keegan's room. She knocked on the door and a voice called us to enter. The room was dimly lit and the priest was seated and facing away, watching television.

I stepped in front of him to introduce myself and my heart sank. It was not my Father Keegan. There was not even one similar facial feature and the piercing blue eyes I remembered were brown. It was an awkward moment and we both realized we had never met before. Small talk was made and I apologized for the intrusion and made my exit.

This was an unexpected setback in my quest for forgiveness. I returned to Hamilton and made more inquiries. It was certainly easier to trace the whereabouts of Father there than from Arizona.

I discovered my Father Keegan had died ten years earlier and any chance of a meeting with him was now just as impossible as meeting with my dad.

It was at that instant I had another moment of clarity:

I had become obsessed with being forgiven for something I had never done wrong. After all, I was just transgender.

I had also become eager to forgive the priest for his harsh judgment of me. But he had not done anything wrong either. He had just been following his training and was a product of the times.

At last, the moment had arrived for me to move on.

Running red lights is something I don't have to contemplate anymore because nothing is holding me back. I can expend my energy in more productive activities, like gardening. At the moment, I have two backyard projects on the go.

The first concerns a Myrtle cactus I planted about twelve years ago. It is a handsome specimen with multiple 'arms' and usually grows to a maximum height of five feet. It adorns itself with dainty white flowers twice a year that attract bees by the thousands.

Under my care, the Myrtle is now ten feet tall! However all is not well because it is starting to lean forward at an alarming angle. The cactus looks at me with a worried expression. Some of its arms are reaching out for my help and I have promised to find a solution.

My second project is planting a new garden. I know the routine so well: Prepare the soil and make sure it has the proper drainage and fertilization. Decide on what to plant given the needs of the family. Watch for favorable weather. Sprinkle the seeds along the orderly rows already arranged. Cover them with some earth, add a little water and wish them good luck. There is no point in growing a new garden if one does not believe in the possibility of a future. Hope is everything.

I did not expect to have dirty hands and be on my knees at the end of my book. So please pardon me if I don't stand up. Given my osteoarthritis, it is difficult to get up and down.

I guess this is the moment where we have to say goodbye. I don't want to make a scene and get all choked-up. I want to say thanks for your company and I hope you enjoyed going on this journey with me. Maybe we can share some new adventures in the future?

In the meantime, I am going to encourage these little seedlings and prepare for their tomorrow. And I'm going to make a concerted effort to smile at the sky a lot more than I have in the past.

Safe travels and have a rich and meaningful life.

Bobbi in her garden, 2017

Comments By The Author

My goal in writing his book was to help as many people as possible. Of course I hope it will be read by transgender individuals and their families and friends. I also dream it will become mandatory reading for healthcare providers, students, golfers, gardeners, faith leaders, advocates and everyone else.

It is a true story, although the older I get my fading memory seems to overlap with dreams. Reality takes on a new meaning.

I have deliberately not provided you with the names of my children and grandchildren because I am protective of them. I have also changed the names of some of the characters to protect their privacy.

Conversations and events that have taken place have been accurately recorded or gently altered for clarity.

I have attempted to adhere to a correct timeline in an effort to allow the story to unfold in a coherent fashion.

Concerning the Science Friday chapter, my intention was not to write a textbook. There is no expectation that any of this story will appear in a medical journal. My goal was to review as many scientific publications as I could, summarize the findings and present them to people who do not have a strong science background. I wanted to provide some basic biology and talk to the public using straightforward language.

There have been many personal transgender stories written. Of course they are all unique and very special. But at times the reader is often left shaking their head as they try to make sense of what motivates a person to change genders. My hope is that this book has answered some of those questions.

I want to comment on the two fathers in my life. One is my biological father otherwise known as Dad. The other is the Father I served as an altar boy. They both died long ago and yet they appear frequently in my thoughts and in my dreams. I had a conflicted relationship with both of them and this book became an opportunity to have a conversation.

The road that led me to reconciliation and forgiveness has been very long and tortuous. I have finally learned it is time to let it be.

Appendix: Question And Answer With Dr. Bobbi

I am frequently asked questions related to being transgender. People recognize I am very candid and approachable and they feel it is safe to explore topics they are curious about but are often too frightened to ask. They don't want to use the wrong terms or pronouns and embarrass themselves or offend the other party.

I thought it might be informative to include some of these questions in this extra section at the end of the book. Many come from students at the conclusion of my presentations. Some come from friends and family.

This first question was asked by a fellow competitor at a recent golf tournament. I was leading the competition by one stroke and the final round was about to commence. As I stood on the first tee, one of the players in the foursome came up to me and offered this zinger:

"Bobbi, given how far you hit the ball and because you were once a guy, do you think it is fair that you are allowed to compete against us?"

This was hardly the time and place to get into this conversation. I knew the competitors quite well and most are friends and very supportive. I did not feel the question was asked to deliberately play with my head, but it was certainly on that fine line called gamesmanship. The others leaned forward to hear my response.

I reminded them that the United States Golf Association had given me permission to compete as a woman so I was not breaking any rules. However, I told them I was concerned about fairness too and was conflicted. I suggested we discuss this further after the round.

I hit a very good opening tee shot about 265 yards. While walking to my ball, I looked back to see where my competitors had driven their balls. I was at least fifty yards ahead of every one of them. I know I was feeling guilty and proceeded to make a mess of the first two holes. Then I settled down and eventually won the event. But the victory felt somewhat hollow. I apologized to the second place finisher who is an incredible player. She dismissed my apology and said it had been a great match and she'd enjoyed the day immensely. Every one congratulated me and they all appeared sincere, but the eight hundred pound 'fairness elephant' occupied most of the room where the awards were presented.

Two weeks later, I played in a one day event. Of course I played from the ladies tees. I drove the 290 yard first hole and made a fifteen foot eagle putt. I drove other par fours too, shot sixty-six and easily won.

Fair?

The issue of fairness as it relates to gender and sport is a complicated topic. Traditionally competitions are divided into all-male or all-female divisions because of the stereotype that men are stronger and faster. But even within each division, there are wide genetic discrepancies in size and athleticism. There is also huge disparity created by factors such as economics and access to the best coaches, psychologists, nutritionists, sports medicine experts, equipment, and competition.

One could argue the mere concept of fairness and a level playing field is an illusion even among cisgender competitors. Adding transgender competitors to the mix just further muddies the water.

The transgender male competing against cisgender males historically has caused very little concern. These transgender men were never exposed to large amounts of testosterone before puberty, so they lack the skeletal structure and muscularity of their cisgender counterparts, no matter how much post-puberty testosterone they take as part of their gender confirmation therapy.

It is the transgender woman like me who cause all the hand-wringing and cries of foul. I did experience a testosterone- fueled puberty and became over six feet tall and well-muscled. I transitioned at sixty years of age and I know the estrogen I now take has weakened me. But has it leveled the playing field enough? I am not sure it has. If I continue to win tournaments against younger cisgender women on a regular basis, then any reasonable person would conclude there is a fairness issue.

If a transgender woman dominated golf competitions, I think a compromise could be arrived at where she would still be welcomed. However, I think she should be handicapped in some way. Shots could be added to her score or she could be asked to play a longer course (this is logistically impractical in a tournament). Or perhaps her victory could have an asterisk beside it and she would share first place with the best cisgender woman. Of course the asterisk would out-her as transgender, but that would be part of the compromise.

Other sports could design their own unique way of handicapping in the spirit of fairness as well.

There are many young people who now come-out as transgender before puberty. If they receive the best medical care, their puberty will be blocked until they reach the age of consent. This means transgender women will never experience a testosterone-fueled puberty and won't acquire the adult male anatomy that would afford them a sports advantage. There will be fewer transgender women that look like me in the future and fairness concerns will disappear.

Major sports organizations, like the International Olympic Committee, need to create better policies to address fairness as it relates to intersex athletes and competitors with non-traditional gender identity.

It's my prediction that in time, competitors will be divided by their testosterone levels and not their gender assigned at birth or their gender identity.

❖   ❖   ❖

*P*aula, a student at the University of Kansas asked, "Dr. Lancaster, do all transgender women require gender- confirmation surgery?" This was a really good question.

"There are people like me who very definitely identify as a woman with no doubt in their mind. And it is in direct conflict with the gender they were assigned at birth. They experience severe dysphoria as a result of the mismatch. I refer to them as *definitely transgender* and I am part of this group. A comprehensive list of therapies is usually required. Gender-confirming surgery is almost always mandatory. Nothing else will alleviate the distress. Unfortunately, some individuals can't afford the surgery or they have co-morbidities that make surgery too risky.

"However there are people who do not feel as certain about their gender identity. In fact they might not identify as belonging to either of the gender choices. They don't appear to have the same degree of mismatch-distress regarding their sense of self and their assigned sex. They call themselves gender-questioning, gender non-conforming, gender-queer and non-binary. These individuals reside somewhere on a spectrum between cisgender and transgender. They grapple with who they are and may present as one sex for a time and then the other. These individuals are not *definitely transgender* and should be very wary of surgical solutions.

"There are also other individuals who are completely content that their gender identity matches their assigned gender at birth. They are not transgender at all, although some observers mistakenly assume they are. It is their gender expression that can be quite confusing to the uninitiated and there are at least sixty terms used to describe them. They may wear cross-gender clothing, or be flamboyant and outrageous or appear androgynous. This group of individuals is clearly not looking for gender-confirmation surgery."

❖ ❖ ❖

*R*ichard, a student at Chandler Gilbert Community College asked me, "Why do you only talk about transgender women? What about transgender men?*

Have you stumbled on any papers that address the biology of why someone is a transgender man?"

I replied, "In the interest of time and because I am a transgender woman, I limit my talk and discuss issues from a transgender woman's point of view. However no slight is intended.

"Of course there are transgender men. Experts originally thought they were a rare phenomenon. But as more people come out in various cultures, it appears about 0.5 % of any given population identify as being transgender. Of those individuals, about 75% are transgender women and 25% are transgender men. These statistics are bound to change.

"Concerning the transgender men, as you know they have XX chromosomes. They have a gene on their X chromosome called CYP17. An even smaller part of that gene is called the CYP17T-34C allele. This tidbit of genetic information programs the handling of their female sex hormones and makes certain they do their job in feminizing the genitalia as well as the brain gender center and everything in between.

"There is evidence that this allele has been lost in a transgender man. Since it is missing, the implication is his female hormone production lacks direction and proper timing. It is not able to exert its customary effect. Not only that, it is well known that all XX individuals produce small amounts of testosterone. In the end, there is too little female hormone to overcome the action of their small amount of testosterone. As a result, it is postulated the brain gender center is masculinized and they identify as men. Once again more research is needed. But we have in this research a valuable piece of genetic information that will, in time, help us fully understand the biological making of a transgender man."

❖ ❖ ❖

A lex, a student at ASU stopped me during my Power Point presentation. He had heard about post-operative regret and an increased suicide rate in transgender women who had undergone gender confirming surgery. He wanted to know more about this.

I replied, "Follow up studies have been published that look at the issue of post-op regret. They clearly indicate that in the vast majority of individuals, there is NO regret. There are examples of regret and poor outcomes in a few individuals who were almost certainly misdiagnosed as transgender when, in fact, they were likely suffering from multiple personality disorder or some other delusional thinking. In those cases, accepted diagnostic criteria and protocols had not been followed. Hopefully in the future there will be objective transgender confirmatory tests to complement the existing subjective psychological tests and help guide everyone involved, avoiding even one case of misdiagnosis and possible regret.

"I do agree that there is significant stress and depression in the post-op transgender women community, not because of regret, but because of discrimination, unemployment, poverty and the lack of family and friend support. Now that is regrettable."

❖ ❖ ❖

*A*lejandro *was another college student who asked, after one of my talks, if I had ever heard of a correlation involving autism and being transgender.* I certainly am not an expert in this area. However, there is recent evidence that children on the autism spectrum are seven times more likely than other young people to be gender-nonconforming.

Dr. John Strang is a pediatric neuropsychologist who is studying this association. This is fascinating stuff and there is so much more to learn.

❖ ❖ ❖

A physician *who attended my talk at an international medical symposium in Manhattan wondered if my discussion about genetics and hormone receptors in my patient called Laura might be useful in trying to understand intersex individuals.*

I responded, "Absolutely. In fact there are multiple conditions that can result in an intersex situation. One of the most common is congenital hyperandrogenism. Aside from this condition, there is another hypothetical pathway that revolves around the concept of hormone insensitivity that I presented earlier.

"Allow me to review. In Laura's case, none of her testosterone hormone receptors were functioning and her development from head to toe defaulted to typical female anatomy. In my case, it is postulated that all of my receptors worked EXCEPT the ones in my brain. So my brain gender center defaulted to typical female anatomy.

"In the intersex individual, it is postulated that all of their receptors function EXCEPT for the ones in the genital area. Without proper hormonal input, the genitals develop into an ambiguous structure.

"While we are on this intersex topic, I want to add a comment. In the past these individuals were assigned their gender at a very young age by well-intentioned physicians and parents. Sadly, there are many examples of disastrous outcomes. This practice is still adhered to all too frequently.

"The most important principle is to 'first, do no harm.' Confirmation surgery should be delayed. This allows time to determine the genetic and hormonal makeup of every situation. Most important, it allows time for the intersex person to reach the age of consent and 'assign' themselves wherever on the gender spectrum they feel situated. They alone will know their gender reality based on how their sense-of-self center was 'wired' during development. Great care must be taken to respect their self-professed gender identity and then appropriate surgeries can follow.

"I only hope the same respect will be given in the future to all individuals, including people like me, who confidently declare their gender identity even if it doesn't match their assigned gender at birth."

Not all of the questions I am asked come from college students. Here is one I received about a year after my transition. I had just finished a round of golf with my old buddies. We were having a drink on the clubhouse patio and there was some cigar smoking going on too. While we were settling our golfing bets, one of my friends took a puff on his cigar, scratched his fairly ample belly and said, "Bobbi, tell me, now that you are taking female hormones and you have had surgery, are you going to start liking guys?"

I watched everyone push back in their chairs a little at the mere thought of me dating men. Maybe men like them?

I replied, "Not a chance, guys. I am attracted to women exclusively and I have been my entire life."

However later that day I thought more about his question and realized it touched upon a very important point.

Gender identity and sexual orientation are two completely separate things and this usually comes as a surprise to the public.

First, gender identify refers to whether a person identifies as a man, a woman, something in between or even no gender at all.

Second, sexual orientation refers to whether a person is attracted to men, women, both or perhaps neither. Approximately seven percent of every population is homosexual. This biological variation does not appear to be influenced by culture or social status. Of course an individual's reported orientation depends on the acceptance in their particular 'neighborhood'.

The areas of the brain that are responsible for gender identity and sexual orientation are located in different anatomical sites. However the developmental wiring of these separate sites appears to be under the same biological controls I have described earlier.

In the case of my gender identity, I was wired with a female sense-of-self. Separately, I have always been sexually attracted to females. I knew this from a young age and neither has changed during my entire life, in spite of the estrogen I am now prescribed. It is difficult to undo or erase firmly entrenched nerve pathways, unless an injury or disease occurs.

I do know several transgender women who were married to women before they transitioned. Now they are attracted to men. Experts suggest they were bisexually wired to begin with. Their sexual orientation was not as firmly at one end of the spectrum as mine.

Lady Gaga is not a biologist but she is absolutely correct when she sings, "I was born this way." Your wiring is not a choice and it is not contagious. The only decision to be made is whether to hide or not.

❖ ❖ ❖

Yet another student at a community college asked me to comment on my experience as a woman and how it differs from my experience when I lived as a man. She was also curious whether people reacted to me differently now.

Here is what I have personally observed: On a superficial note, I now have doors held open for me and I am asked if I need help to my car with the groceries. There are courtesies extended to me that are unexpected and quite charming. They often catch me off-guard. It seems there is an assumption I am weak and can't handle certain things.

I notice that women who are complete strangers will smile and acknowledge me as I walk down the street or shop at a store. I feel like I have been accepted into some informal sisterhood and it feels really good.

I also notice that, in general, men are loud. They take up a lot of space. I did not notice this when I was living as a man.

Aside from these rather harmless observations, I do have some concerns. When I make a comment at a meeting, I have to really speak loudly because otherwise I am unnoticed. This never happened when I presented as Dr. Bob. I feel like I am invisible now at times.

I also have male friends who feel free to comment on my wardrobe and my hair. They have encouraged me to never wear certain golf outfits again because they were "inappropriate, unflattering or perhaps made me look fat." They suggest I should dress more "in-keeping with my age." Criticisms like these were never offered when I was Bob.

Also when I play golf as a single and am asked to join a group of male golfers, I sense a collective groan. There is an assumption I will slow them down or spoil their day. Of course in my case, that sentiment disappears as soon as I hit my first shot forty yards past their best tee shots.

Being aware of the fact that men stare at me and sometimes whistle, I am careful to watch where I am because I sense a certain vulnerability or even danger that I never experienced before.

In summary, as a woman I am perceived to be weak and insignificant. I feel like I am being judged and compared. This is called good old-fashioned sexism with a little misogyny thrown in for good measure. It is a pathetic fact that my slim, athletic and attractive presentation have contributed greatly to my successful transition. I'll leave it to sociologists and much smarter people to more thoroughly comment on my observations.

❖   ❖   ❖

I received this question from an attendee at a White House Summit discussing transgender issues. I was on a panel.

"Dr. Lancaster, first....do you feel that being transgender is like having a disease or an illness? And second, if it was available, would you agree to some treatment that would alter your brain gender center so you could identify as a male and avoid the dysphoria you lived with?"

Let's look at the first part of the question. Do I consider being transgender akin to having a disease or an illness? In my opinion I don't think it rises to that level. However the affected individuals generally require counseling, psychologists, medication, cross gender hormones, puberty blockers, speech therapy, electrolysis, laser therapy and multiple complicated surgeries. Given all of the interventions that are necessary, they obviously have some sort of medical condition probably best described as a syndrome, rather than a disease.

In fact let's call it Gender Identity Syndrome. This would allow for its placement in medical textbooks. It could be included in the chapter that discusses complete androgen insensitivity syndrome, intersex states, and other related conditions. Its causation, prevalence, diagnostic criteria, confirmatory tests, differential diagnosis, treatment, side effects and prognosis could all be discussed.

I think this would promote better public understanding and acceptance of the transgender individual. It would hopefully put more pressure on insurance companies to cover the medically necessary treatments for their transition. Perhaps it would help encourage more research interest.

At the present time in this country, this condition is only officially listed in psychiatric manuals and is called gender dysphoria. Yes, there is a state of feeling unwell but this is simply a descriptive term that trivializes the issue. It encourages continued raised eyebrows and marginalization of the transgender population.

As an aside, I am looking forward to some feedback concerning my use of the word syndrome. I predict there will be taxonomists who are going to jump all over me. It should be interesting.

Now, I'll address the second part of your question. If there was some therapy that would allow me to identify as a male, would I accept the treatment?

Well if you are talking about changing my brain gender center wiring during childhood, adolescence or later, that is called conversion therapy. This 'treatment' basically involves administering very uncomfortable stimuli as part of a negative psychological conditioning program that would force me to conform to my birth gender. I call it sadistic; to me it is basically torture.

Studies indicate these techniques are bogus and do not work. They also have done great psychological harm to many individuals and side effects can be life-threatening. Every major medical association has spoken out and condemned these so-called conversion therapies

Now if you are talking about a theoretical treatment that could be administered to me in-utero that would modify brain development and avoid my future gender identity syndrome, would I accept it? Heck no.

First of all, I would be petrified of unintended consequences. I cringe at the thought of introducing some genetic or hormonal treatment into an embryo in the hope of preventing future gender identity issues. And any study or therapeutic trial of this imagined therapy would be blatantly unethical.

As a final thought, why would it be desirable to change individuals like me? I am unique and have great worth. I contribute to society in many ways. Do we really want to get rid of diversity for the sake of making everyone more the same? What would be the real and intangible cost if we could accomplish such a cleansing?

Yes, I would like the symptoms related to my gender identity syndrome treated, thank you very much. Otherwise leave me alone because I have a life to live.

❖ ❖ ❖

*A*t the end of my talk at a local community college, one of the professors stood up and asked me, "Dr. Lancaster, some of my students want to explore the many topics you have introduced. Can you provide them with the names of experts you have come across during the writing of this book?"

I replied, "Well of course. The following is a list of scientists who are well published in peer-reviewed journals and they will open up the world of gender research to your students:

- Jiang–Ning Zhou, PhD in Neurobiology. University of Science and Technology, China.
- Louis J. Gooren, MD, Professor of Endocrinology, Vrije University, Amsterdam.
- Dick F. Swaab, Netherland Institute for Neurosciences.
- F.P.M. Kruijver, MD, Netherland Institute for Brain Research.
- Julianne Imperato-McGinley, Weill Cornell Medical College.

- Georgiann Davis, University of Nevada, Las Vegas.
- John Strang, Children's National Health System, Washington, D.C.
- Eric Vilain, UCLA Center for Gender Based Biology.
- Jean Malpas, Ackerman Institute for the Family in New York City.
- Norman P. Spack, MD, Boston Children's Hospital.

"Also, have them check out the January 2017 publication of National Geographic. It was called the Gender Revolution and it was followed by a beautifully produced documentary hosted by Katie Couric.

"I would also encourage them to Google 'causes of transsexualism' and see where Wikipedia takes them. Beware of the haters. Let science be your guide.

"Finally here are several transgender memoirs that are well written. I think your students would enjoy them:

- She's Not There, by Jennifer Finney Boylan.
- My Brother My Sister, by Molly Haskell.
- Wrapped in Blue, by Donna Rose.
- Getting to Ellen, by Ellen Krug

"There is also an excellent book called The Whipping Girl by Julia Serano. She is a scholar and speaks knowledgeably about sexism and transphobia.

"This list is not meant to be comprehensive. However, it will be a start for your students as they pursue a better understanding of gender in all of its complexity."

❖   ❖   ❖

*F*inally, a small group of psychology students approached me after a talk. One of them stepped forward, blushed and said she wanted to ask me a question about a sensitive topic. She said she would understand if I did not want to answer.

I knew right away what the question would be because it has been asked frequently at the end of encounters by embarrassed interviewers, reporters, students and friends. It concerns my sex life.

They all know my wife and I have remained married even after my transition and this is unusual in itself, but not unheard of. They are curious about how we navigated the intimacy in our relationship now that I am changed anatomically.

Of course I tell them every couple like us will have their own story to tell. In our case, there is no sexual intimacy anymore. Lucy is very clearly heterosexually wired and she does not find my new body attractive in the least.

At that point the questioner usually looks a little sad and I tell them there is nothing to fret over. On the contrary, we enjoy an incredibly caring relationship based on love, respect and mutual admiration. We hold hands, sit close, talk about everything and dream of our future. There are constant shows of affection and a frequently spoken refrain: "I love you" and "I love you more."

Perhaps we are not joined sexually anymore but we are very powerfully joined 'at the heart' and this is more than enough to see us through.

"Thanks for having the courage to ask the question that everyone else is nervously dying to ask."

Acknowledgements

I am indebted to the incredible editing skills of Anthea Penne, an award-winning author from Canada. Her attention to detail and gentle handling of my fragile ego were invaluable. She repeatedly told me my storytelling held great promise and urged me to push forward. She never stopped believing and assisted me to the finish line.

I also am grateful for my friend and occasional caddy, Gerry Byrne. He was the first to read my very rough initial draft and his insights and suggestions were jolting. In the end they proved to be extremely helpful and the book is better because of Gerry. We remain good friends.

I also have to thank my friend, Sheila Kloefkorn. We had met for coffee to discuss LGBTQ advocacy when, out of the blue, she suggested I write a book. She planted the seed and instructed me to simply follow the format of the talks I present at schools and conventions. I quickly learned that delivering a speech and writing a book are radically different exercises. With

Sheila's support, I accomplished what initially appeared to be a monumental task.

I must thank my mom, Rosalie, my sister Sandy and my brothers, Ron and Ken. They were understandably apprehensive I might reveal uncomfortable secrets that every family harbors. In the end, they made significant contributions to the book and are proud the Lancaster story is being told through my eyes.

I am also fortunate to have received love and support from my children, grandchildren and my first wife, Mary Jo. It has been an equally challenging journey for them as well.

The rest of the list of grateful acknowledgements is unending because it spans my entire life:

There are my childhood friends Crystal, Mary, Virgilio, Rocco and Joe with whom I shared dreams and secrets.

There are my early golf buddies, Garry Gibson, Bob and John Wynne, Howard Brock, Zinger, Norm Hitzroth, Rusty Baker, Jeff Howlett and Brent Loutit. Our rivalries and little money games were legendary. College teammates included Doug Rosart, Dave Moser, Brian Hoyle, Paul Donegle and Ian Giles. Doug bestowed upon me the nickname of Eustice for some inexplicable reason when I was captain of the team. He still calls me by that name to this day.

Dick Borthwick was the long-standing head professional at Hamilton Golf and Country Club. I shagged balls for him endlessly and tried to emulate his swing.

He gave me his set of Wilson Staff woods after I caddied for him as a young teen. This was a huge gesture and very much appreciated. He passed away years ago. Eventually Gary Maue became the head pro and he was very supportive. He invited me to be the guest speaker at the annual caddy banquet one year. This was an honor I will cherish forever.

There was Rod Goodes, the head professional at Chedoke Civic Golf Course for many years. Back in the early seventies, he hired me to work in the pro shop and I'd use his car to visit the golf equipment companies in Toronto once a week, on his behalf. I practiced my driving during those trips. Thankfully he never found out about the abuse I put his red car through for several summers. He never questioned the need for new rear tires every few months.

I did not discuss my love of sports cars in this book. My close friends will all attest to the parade of exotic cars I have owned throughout the years and there are hair-raising stories of my exuberant speeding back in the day. My best car friend was Doug Smith. He recently passed and I am still actively grieving this loss.

I must thank several of my most memorable teachers. They include Sister Prisca, Dr. Vince Rudnick, and Dr. Ron McAuley. They are all deceased. Dr. Paul O'Byrne was my Chief Resident during my internship and I adopted his problem solving technique and charting style that I still use to this day.

It's time to acknowledge my current friends, in no particular order. They are Roy Hardick, Abe Dye, Randy Williams, Nina and Loren Valencia, Mike Brown, Karen Pultz, Alena Sharp, Sarah Bowman, Ava Lourenco, Dom Dinallo, Dr. John Chong, Noelle Nicolas, Ashley Burrill, Marilynn Smith, Shellie and Randi Ruge, Justin Jones, Kent Couchee, Tiana Hammond, Hailey Davidson, Heather Daly-Donofrio, Sophia Mayberry, Sue Weiger, Terese Cullen and Julie Stimple. There are too many acquaintances and patients to even begin to list. They will be disappointed I did not mention their names. However each and every one of them enriched my life and helped me through.

There is a host of medical professionals who helped me navigate the many health challenges I've faced. The list includes Dr. Toby Meltzer, Chris Dorris, Dr. Ian Strickland, Denae Doyle, Mary Brasch, Dr. Jennifer Lewis, Dr. Ken Fisher, Carol Williams NP, Dr. Mike Brennan, Dr. Schulte, Pete Berger, Dr. Peter Maki, Dr. James Frey, Dr. Belinda Barclay-White, Dr. Ashish Pershad, Maria DeNicola, Bob and Kristin Graving, to name a few. I trusted all of them and placed my very life in their capable hands. I am truly grateful for their help.

My transition to life as Dr. Bobbi and my foray into professional golf resulted in interest from the international media. I will be forever appreciative of the sensitive and professional manner in which the journalists presented my story. The thank-you list includes Paola

Boivin (AZ Republic), Jimmy Roberts and Ryan Griffiths (NBC Sports/Golf Channel), Cheryl Evans (AZ Republic), Kevin Kennedy and Bryan West (Channel 12 News), Jered Stuffco(Canadian Medical Post), Mia Sheldon (Global News), Nigel Campbell (Instinct Magazine), Gary Trost (TMZ), Huffpost, KJ Philp (Echo Magazine), Randy Boswell (Canadian Post Media), John Moore (CFRB Toronto), Clea Kim (Advocate.com), Aaron McQuade (GLAAD), Bill Van Nimwegen (Apache Junction News), Pete Madden, Lucas O'Neill and Marika Washchyshyn (Sports Illustrated/ Golf), Ken Reed (League of Fans), Michael Lacey (New Times), Allyson Rowley (McMaster Times), Adam Polaski (Freedom for All Americans), Kaly Nasiff and Haley Bosselman (Cronkite School of Journalism). I am sorry if I have left some journalists off this list.

Finally I have to acknowledge my wife Lucy. She has been tireless in her support of this book and has endured repeated questions like, "Honey, when you have a minute, can you come and listen to how I have revised this chapter? What do you think of this phrasing? Do you think the reader will be confused by this? Do you know how to spell whatever? Should there be a comma here or not?"

She never once lost her patience because she understood how important this project was to me. Thank you Lucy and I'll love you forever.

I have come to realize there should be a special place reserved for the spouse of any writer.

Photo by Joanne West

About the Author

D r. Bobbi Lancaster is a family physician who lives in Gold Canyon, Arizona. She is most proud of the care she has delivered to her patients for almost forty years.

She shares a wonderful life with her wife Lucy; they are the best of friends. Bobbi is also thrilled to be the parent of three grown children and "Papa" to her two grandchildren.

She enjoys writing, gardening, staying fit and caring for all creatures, great and small. Her golf skills are eroding due to age and lack of play. However she is really enjoying teaching the game to her grandkids. It is almost certain golf in some capacity will play a role in her life forever.

Bobbi has big plans for the future. She will continue to speak out against transgender discrimination and work for understanding, acceptance and equality. She is changing hearts and minds one person at a time with her very personal and genuine approach.

Bobbi plans to continue writing and perhaps adventure into poetry. She also wants to shake the dust off her old piano skills and feel the beat again. Bobbi hopes to reconnect with her beloved butterflies and take the public on tours at a local arboretum. In her opinion, butterflies represent everything beautiful, gentle and mysterious about life. The world needs more butterflies.

Bobbi regrets never learning another language and traveling more. She also laments never once trying to jump rope, especially Double Dutch.

Aside from this, she really enjoys helping Lucy with her hobby of raising and training companion dogs. As the principle poop scooper, Bobbi likes to say it keeps her grounded.

She encourages you to connect with her on Facebook and through Twitter. She can also be reached at plusoneatsixty@hotmail.com.

Made in the USA
Columbia, SC
29 March 2018